Come Follow Me

Foundations for Your Relationship with God

Will & Jaime Riddle

Part One: Knowing God

Part Two: Obeying God

Part Three: Walking with God

GETTING STARTED

This book is designed to put your walk with God onto a firm foundation. Whether you just gave your life to Jesus for the first time, or you are rededicating your life to Him, the goal is the same: to help you to walk closely with Jesus every day.

The lessons in this book are designed to guide you in your relationship with God. When you gave your life to Jesus, you were not promised facts or an interesting book with good rules to live by. You were promised a relationship with God.

Your progress in God is based on what is inside your heart. The goal of this book is to help you cultivate your heart so you can come to know Jesus closely and personally.

The lessons in this book are designed to be practical. It is one thing to know the right thing to believe, but it is even more important to know the right thing to do.

The lessons in this book come right out of the Bible. The way you see the Bible has a huge effect on the way you see God and the way you live your life. When life and sin confuse you and move you off the path, the Bible is one thing that does not change. We present Scriptures from the Bible and then ask you questions designed to help you see and understand the importance of what those verses teach. We have copied Bible passages directly into this book to make it easier to study, but we of course encourage you to read more in your own Bible as you go.

Thank you so much for coming on this journey with us! Now, let's follow Jesus!

PART I:
KNOWING GOD

GOD'S LOVE

What is God Like?

God is love. (1 John 4:16)

The Bible does not just say God is loving. It says God is love. What is the difference?

_____

_____

Can you imagine what it would be like to know someone who was completely loving all the time? Describe what it would be like.

_____

_____

_____

You have heard that it was said, 'Love your neighbor and hate your enemy.' But I tell you: Love your enemies and pray for those who persecute you, that you may be sons of your Father in heaven. He causes his sun to rise on the evil and the good, and sends rain on the righteous and the unrighteous. If you love those who love you, what reward will you get?... Your Heavenly Father is perfect. (Matthew 5:43-48)

Does God only love those who love Him?

_____

What is God's attitude toward those who curse Him?

_____

Is this just an attitude, or does He actually do nice things for them? What two examples does Jesus give?

_____

Those are just general examples. Can you imagine any other practical ways that God might show love or bless those that hate Him?

_____

_____

Regardless of whether you have loved him or hated Him, what is God's attitude toward you?

_____

_____

Have you ever done anything really wrong? According to this passage, what was God's attitude toward you while you were doing it?

_____

_____

There was a man who had two sons. The younger one said to his father, "Father, give me my share of the estate." So he divided his property between them. Not long after that, the younger son got together all he had, set off for a distant country and there squandered his wealth in wild living. After he had spent everything, there was a severe famine in that whole country, and he began to be in need. So he went and hired himself out to a citizen of that country, who sent him to his fields to feed pigs. He longed to fill his stomach with the pods that the pigs were eating, but no one gave him anything.

When he came to his senses, he said, "How many of my father's hired men have food to spare, and here I am starving to death! I will set out and go back to my father and say to him: 'Father, I have sinned against heaven and against you. I am no longer worthy to be called your son; make me like one of your hired men.'" So he got up and went to his father.

But while he was still a long way off, his father saw him and was filled with compassion for him. He ran to his son, threw his arms around him and kissed him. The son said to him, "Father, I have sinned against heaven and against you. I am no longer worthy to be called your son." But the father said to his servants, "Quick! Bring the best robe and put it on him. Put a ring on his finger and sandals on his feet. Bring the fattened calf and kill it. Let's have a feast and celebrate. For this son of mine was dead and is alive again; he was lost and is found." So they began to celebrate. (Luke 15:11-24)

The father in this story represents God. The son represents those who are living selfishly. At first how did the son treat the Father?

_____

_____

How did the father treat the son back? Was he mean at any time?

_____

_____

When the son returned, did the father wait to see what the son's attitude was before he showed love to him?

_____

What does this say about the father's love for the son?

_____

Based on how the father responded when the son came back, how do you think the father felt while his son was far away, living the party life?

_____

Even though the father loved the son unconditionally, what step did the son have to take in order to restore the relationship?

_____

God will always love you even if are far away from Him, but what step do we take in order to relate to Him and feel His love back?

_____

Love is patient. Love is kind. It does not envy, it does not boast, it is not proud. It is not rude. It is not self-seeking. It is not easily angered. It keeps no record of wrongs. Love does not delight in evil but rejoices with the truth. It always protects, always trusts, always hopes, always perseveres. Love never fails. (1 Corinthians 13:4-8)

This is how the Bible defines love. Since God loves you, describe what His attitude is toward you.

_____

Is God patient with you when you make a mistake?

_____

When you are rude or selfish, how does God treat you?

_____

Does God keep a record of your wrongs?

_____

Will God protect you?

_____

Does God trust you?

_____

Based on all of this, what kind of person do you think Jesus is?

_____

Does this description of Jesus differ from anything you have believed about Him in the past? If so, how?

_____

_____

_____

> They asked Him, "Teacher, which is the greatest commandment in the Law?" Jesus replied: "'Love the Lord your God with all your heart and with all your soul and with all your mind.' This is the first and greatest commandment. And the second is like it: 'Love your neighbor as yourself.' All the Law and the Prophets hang on these two commandments." (Matthew 22:36-40)

The Bible has many instructions, but according to Jesus, what summarizes the heart behind all these instructions?

_____

_____

When God tells you not to do something, what is His motivation behind it?

_____

_____

If all of God's laws are based on love, what do you think is the goal of everything God does?

_____

_____

We love because He first loved us. (1 John 4:19)

What do you have to receive in your heart before you can truly love God or others?

_____

For God so loved the world that He gave His one and only Son, that whoever believes in Him shall not perish but have everlasting life. For God did not send his Son into the world to condemn the world but to save the world through Him. (John 3:16-17)

What was God's motivation to send Jesus to die for you?

_____

Does God want to send people to hell? How can you tell?

_____

_____

When we were still God's enemies, we were reconciled to Him through the death of his Son (Romans 5:10).

Did Jesus die for you because you were good enough?

_____

Imagine someone who hates you. Now imagine a person whom you love with your whole heart. Can you imagine sending the one whom you love to their death? Would you send them to die in order to save the life of the one who hates you? What does this say about the kind of love God has for you?

_____

_____

_____

God's kindness leads you toward repentance. (Romans 2:4)

Does God use cruel punishments or threats to make you love Him? What does He use instead?

_____

What is the result of allowing God's love into your life?

_____

Why do you think God wants you to repent? How does this show He loves you?

_____

Having a Receptive Heart

A farmer went out to sow his seed. As he was scattering the seed, some fell along the path, and the birds came and ate it up. Some fell on rocky places, where it did not have much soil. It sprang up quickly, because the soil was shallow. But when the sun came up, the plants were scorched, and they withered because they had no root. Other seed fell among thorns, which grew up and choked the plants. Still other seed fell on good soil, where it produced a crop – a hundred, sixty or thirty times what was sown. He who has ears, let him hear...

Listen then to what the parable of the sower means: When anyone hears the message about the kingdom and does not understand it, the evil one comes and snatches away what was sown in his heart. This is the seed sown along the path. The one who received the seed that fell on rocky places is the man who hears the word and at once receives it with joy. But since he has no root, he lasts only a short time. When trouble or persecution comes because of the word, he quickly falls away. The one who received the seed that fell among the thorns is the man who hears the word, but the worries of this life and the deceitfulness of wealth choke it, making it unfruitful.

But the one who received the seed that fell on good soil is the man who hears the word and understands it. He produces a crop, yielding a hundred, sixty or thirty times what was sown.

Think about the process of growing a plant from a seed, to bearing fruit. How long does this take?

_____

What kind of steps are involved in cultivating a plant long enough to bear fruit?

_____

_____

What kinds of obstacles does Jesus say a plant will face before it reaches maturity?

_____

_____

If the "seed" represents God's truth, and the "soil" represents your heart, what two things do you need to grow strong in God's Kingdom?

_____

_____

Based on this passage, is following God is supposed to be easy?

_____

Who comes to distract you whenever you hear the truth?

_____

Some people hear the truth and start down the right path but give up following God. Why do they quit?

_____

_____

Some people keep the truth in their hearts, yet do not bear any fruit. Why not?

_____

According to this passage, in order to survive and bear fruit, you must have deep roots. How can you prepare your own heart to have the roots go deep?

_____

_____

Building a Solid Foundation

Everyone who hears these words of mine and puts them into practice is like a wise man who built his house on the rock. The rain came down, the streams rose, and the winds blew and beat against that house; yet it did not fall, because it had its foundation on the rock. But everyone who hears these words of mine and does not put them into practice is like a foolish man who built his house on sand. The rain came down, the streams rose, and the winds blew and beat against that house, and it fell with a great crash. (Matthew 7:24-27)

In this passage, building your life on Jesus and His teachings is compared to what?

_____

What will happen to your life if you do not build on Jesus' words?

_____

_____

What are the two components of building your house on the Rock?

_____

_____

If you build on Jesus, will you still have storms?

_____

If you build on Jesus, will your house prevail?

_____

Why is Bible study important?

_____

_____

THE FATHER'S DESIRE FOR RELATIONSHIP

Created for Relationship

In the beginning was the Word, and the Word was with God, and the Word was God. He was with God in the beginning. Through him all things were made; without him nothing was made that has been made. In him was life, and that life was the light of all mankind. (John 1:1-4)

When God the Father created the world, was He alone?

_____

Jesus said... "Father, glorify me in your presence with the glory I had with you before the world began." (John 17:5)

Who was with God before the world was created?

_____

What does it sound like their relationship was like?

_____

Then God said, "Let us make mankind in our image, in our likeness..." (Genesis 1:26)

Who does the "us" refer to when God created the world?

_____

Why do you think God wanted to create mankind? Does He want a relationship with you?

_____

_____

If God existed in relationship and created mankind out of that relationship, to be made in His image—what does that say about your need for relationship?

_____

The Lord God said, "It is not good for man to be alone. I will make a helper suitable for him." (Genesis 2:18-23)

Everything God created he said was "good" except that Adam had no human companion. What does that say about how important God thinks relationship is?

_____

Did Adam have to take care of his own needs? Who saw what his relational needs were and took care of them?

_____

Separation from God

And the LORD God commanded the man, "You are free to eat from any tree in the garden; but you must not eat from the tree of the knowledge of good and evil, for when you eat from it you will certainly die."

Now the serpent was more crafty than any of the wild animals the LORD God had made. He said to the woman, "Did God really say, 'You must not eat from any tree in the garden'?"

The woman said to the serpent, "We may eat fruit from the trees in the garden, but God did say, 'You must not eat fruit from the tree that is in the middle of the garden, and you must not touch it, or you will die.'"

"You will not certainly die," the serpent said to the woman. "For God knows that when you eat from it your eyes will be opened, and you will be like God, knowing good and evil."

When the woman saw that the fruit of the tree was good for food and pleasing to the eye, and also desirable for gaining wisdom, she took some and ate it. She also gave some to her husband, who was with her, and he ate it. Then the eyes of both of them were opened, and they realized they were naked; so they sewed fig leaves together and made coverings for themselves. Then the man and his wife heard the sound of the LORD God as he was walking in the garden in the cool of the day, and they hid from the LORD God among the trees of the garden.

But the LORD God called to the man, "Where are you?" (Genesis 2:16-17,3:1-8)

If God was "walking" with Adam in the Garden of Eden, what does this show about their relationship, originally?

_____

If Eve doubted what God told them, what does that tell you about her trust in God and in His relationship with them?

_____

_____

If Adam listened to Eve and doubted what God had told him, what does that tell you about his trust?

_____

_____

What happened to Adam and Eve's relationship with God as a result of their disobedience?

_____

_____

How did Adam and Eve's feelings change about relating to God?

_____

_____

How did God respond when the relationship was suddenly broken?

_____

_____

Enoch Walks with God

When Enoch had lived 65 years, he became the father of Methuselah. After he became the father of Methuselah, Enoch walked faithfully with God 300 years and had other sons and daughters. Altogether, Enoch lived a total of 365 years. Enoch walked faithfully with God; then he was no more, because God took him up. (Genesis. 5:21-24)

Why did God take Enoch to heaven?

_____

What does this say about God felt about Enoch?

_____

_____

How does this remind you of the Garden of Eden?

_____

_____

If Enoch fellowshipped with God on earth, what do you think Enoch did with Him in heaven?

_____

What does this suggest is the most important aspect of heaven?

_____

What does this suggest is the most important thing to God?

_____

Abraham Dialogues with God

Abram lived in the land of Canaan, while Lot lived among the cities of the plain and pitched his tents near Sodom. Now the people of Sodom were wicked and were sinning greatly against the Lord... Then the Lord said, "Shall I hide from Abraham what I am about to do? Abraham will surely become a great and powerful nation, and all nations on earth will be blessed through him. For I have chosen him so that he will direct his children and his household after him to keep the way of the Lord by doing what is right and just, so that the Lord will bring about for Abraham what he has promised him." Then the Lord said, "The outcry against Sodom and Gomorrah is so great and their sin so grievous that I will go down and see if what they have done is as bad as the outcry that has reached me. If not, I will know."

God knew Abraham cared about Sodom. Did God hide it from him?

_____

Why didn't God hide it from him? What was God trying to keep?

_____

The men turned away and went toward Sodom, but Abraham remained standing before the Lord. Then Abraham approached him and said: "Will you sweep away the righteous with the wicked? What if there are fifty righteous people in the city? Will you really sweep it away and not spare the place for the sake of the fifty righteous people in it? Far be it from you to do such a thing—to kill the righteous with the wicked, treating the righteous and the wicked alike. Far be it from you! Will not the Judge of all the earth do right?" The Lord said, "If I find fifty righteous people in the city of Sodom, I will spare the whole place for their sake."

Then Abraham spoke up again: "Now that I have been so bold as to speak to the Lord, though I am nothing but dust and ashes, what if the number of the righteous is five less than fifty? Will you destroy the whole city for lack of five people?" "If I find forty-five there," the Lord said, "I will not destroy it." Once again he spoke to him, "What if only forty are found there?" He said, "For the sake of forty, I will not do it." Then he said, "May the Lord not be angry, but let me speak. What if only thirty can be found there?" He answered, "I will not do it if I find thirty there." Abraham said, "Now that I have been so bold as to speak to the Lord, what if only twenty can be found there?" He said, "For the sake of twenty, I will not destroy it."

Then he said, "May the Lord not be angry, but let me speak just once more. What if only ten can be found there?" He answered, "For the sake of ten, I will not destroy it." When the Lord had finished speaking with Abraham, he left, and Abraham returned home. (Genesis 13:8-13; 18:16-33)

What was Abraham doing when he began a dialogue with the Lord?

_____

How did Abraham feel about doing this?

_____

How many times did Abraham continue to ask God to change His mind?

_____

How did the Lord respond to this asking?

_____

What kind of relationship does the interaction between God and Abraham show that they had?

_____

What kind of relationship does God want you, as a child of Abraham, to have with Him?

_____

Will He be upset when you speak to him, or ask for things on your heart?

_____

> And Abraham believed God, and it was reckoned to him as righteousness, and he was called the friend of God. (James 2:23)

What word does the Bible use to describe Abraham's relationship with God?

_____

What was the main thing that made God draw close to Abraham?

_____

> "I no longer call you servants, because a servant does not know his master's business. Instead, I have called you friends, for everything that I learned from my Father I have made known to you. You did not choose me, but I chose you and appointed you so that you might go and bear fruit—fruit that will last—and so that whatever you ask in my name the Father will give you."   (John 15:15-16)

What does Jesus call you?

_____

What is God's promise to you, if you set yourself to do His will?

_____

In the space of about a chapter, God says three times to ask Him for what you need (John 15:7, 15:16, and 16:23-24). What kind of parent would encourage you to continually ask for things so that they can give them to you?

_____

What do you think God imagined would come from His giving you what you ask?

_____

Moses and Joshua

Thus the Lord used to speak to Moses face to face, just as a man speaks to his friend... When Moses returned to the camp, his servant Joshua, the son of Nun, a young man, would not depart from the tent." (Exodus 33:11)

What word does the Bible use to describe how God desired to talk to Moses?

_____

How do you speak to your friends? How would your life change if you spoke to God like this?

_____

_____

God initiated this relationship with Moses to tell the secrets of how to draw Israel close to Him. What does this say about how God feels about His people?

_____

_____

What did Joshua learn from watching Moses?

_____

Was friendship with God reserved specifically just for one special man?

_____

Jesus' Desire to Befriend Us

I will pray to the Father, and He shall give you another Comforter, that He may abide with you forever. (John 14:16)

Of all the things God could have given us, He chose to give the Holy Spirit to "comfort" us. What does this say about God?

_____

The Holy Spirit is not just a gift. He is God himself. This means who is really doing the comforting?

_____

> Oh Jerusalem, Jerusalem, you who kill the prophets and stone those sent to you, how often I have longed to gather your children together, as a hen gathers her chicks under her wings, and you were not willing. (Luke 13:34)

What kind of a relationship does a hen have with her chicks?

_____

What is this saying about God's feelings towards us?

_____

_____

Jesus said this at a time when He was feeling frustrated and angry towards the Pharisees who resisted Him. This means that when we sin and resist God, what is He hoping we will do?

_____

Who runs from relationship—God, or us?

_____

> Jesus wept. (John 11:35)

This is one of the most famous verses in the Bible, which Jesus does right after He finds his friend, Lazarus, has died. What does Jesus' crying tell us about His nature?

_____

_____

Is He feeling or unfeeling?

_____

Jesus mourned because He felt His own grief, and people's grief surrounding the death of their friend. What does this tell us about how God feels when we are hurting, or when someone dies?

_____

And I, John, saw the holy city, New Jerusalem, coming down from God out of Heaven, prepared as a bride adorned for her husband... "Come here and I will show you the bride, the wife of the Lamb." (Revelation 21:2, 9)

God compares eternity to a wedding. If He is going to marry us forever, how does He feel about us?

How does a good husband treat his wife in times of difficulty and disappointments?

How will God treat you when you are going through difficult times?

Drawing Close to the Father

As the Father has loved me, so have I loved you. Now remain in my love. (John 15:9)

Is it just Jesus who loves you? Where did Jesus' love for you come from?

If you keep my commands, you will remain in my love, just as I have kept my Father's commands and remain in his love. I have told you this so that my joy may be in you and that your joy may be complete. My command is this: Love each other as I have loved you. Greater love has no one than this: to lay down one's life for one's friends. You are my friends if you do what I command. (John 15:10-14)

Why did Jesus command us to love one another?

What happens if we obey that command?

_____

_____

Everything the Father is doing is because He loves you. What is the sign that He loves you with everything He has?

_____

Is the Son willing to be part of this plan? How does He feel about it?

_____

> I tell you the truth; it is better that I go away for if I do not go away, the Helper will not come to you. But if I go, I will send him to you...When the Spirit of truth comes, he will guide you into all the truth, for he will not speak on his own authority but whatever he hears he will speak, and he will declare to you the things that are to come. He will glorify me, for he will take what is mine and declare it to you. All that the Father has is mine; therefore I said that he will take what is mine and declare it to you. (John 16:7, 13-15)

Does God want you to be left alone?

_____

What about God Himself? Does He want to be alone? How can you tell?

_____

Does the Father want any secrets between Himself and you?

_____

Does the Father want to hold back anything from you?

_____

> In that day, you will ask in my name and I do not say that I will ask the Father on your behalf; for the Father himself loves you because you have loved me and have believed that I came from God.   (John 16:26-27)

Can you pray to the Father for what you need?

_____

Do you have to worry that He is angry with you, for any reason?

_____

Does Jesus need to change the Father's mind, to keep his wrath from you?

_____

I do not ask for these only but also for those who will believe in my through their word, that they may all be one just as you, Father, are in me, and I in you, that they also may be in us, so that the world may believe that you have sent me. The glory that you have given me, I have given to them so that they may be one even as we are one. I in them and you in me, that they may become perfectly one, so that the world may know that you sent me and loved them even as you loved me. Father, I desire that they whom you have given me may also be with me where I am, to see my glory that you have given me because you loved me before the foundation of the world...I will continue to make it know that the love with which you have loved me may be in them, and I in them." (John 17:20-26).

Does Jesus make any distinctions between Himself, the Father, and us? Are we supposed to be separated in any way?

_____

What is the main emotion circulating between God and us?

_____

Where does Jesus ask for us to be able to live?

_____

_____

Does God want close relationship? How close?

_____

_____

Draw near to God and He will draw near to you. (James 4:8)

If you want God to be close to you, what should you do?

_____

JESUS SAVES YOU
The Reality of Sin

For all have sinned and fall short of the glory of God. (Romans 3:23)

What is our true destiny? Why can't we reach it?

_____

_____

As it is written, "there is no-one righteous, not even one; there is no-one who understands; there is no-one who seeks God." (Romans 3:11)

According to the Bible, is there such thing as a truly "good person?"

_____

For the wages of sin is death, but the gift of God is eternal life in Christ Jesus our Lord. (Romans 6:23)

How do "wages" normally work?

_____

_____

Why do you think God describes sin like "wages"?

_____

_____

What is the ultimate consequence of sin?

_____

_____

Is God happy about this situation? How can you tell?

_____

But God demonstrates His own love for us in this: while we were still sinners, Christ died for us. (Romans 5:8)

Does God hate you because you have sinned?

_____

What was His response to sin?

_____

The Returning Son

[The son] got up and came to his father. But while he was still a long way off, his father saw him and felt compassion for him, and ran and embraced him and kissed him. And the son said to him, "Father, I have sinned against heaven and in your sight; I am no longer worthy to be called your son." But the father said to his slaves, "Quickly, bring out the best robe and put it on him, and put a ring on his hand and sandals on his feet; and bring the fattened calf, kill it, and let us eat and celebrate; for this son of mine was dead and has come to life again; he was lost and has been found." And they began to celebrate. (Luke 15:19-24)

As a rich man, the father in this story has all he needs. But what is he missing? Why does it matter most?

_____

_____

The fattened calf would have been a farmer's prize possession. How willing is the father, to sacrifice it for the renewed fellowship?

_____

Does the father want to punish his lost son? Or to forgive him?

_____

Does the father want to think about what the son did? Or celebrate his new choice?

_____

What matters most to your heavenly Father, about you?

_____

Remember that you were at that time separated from Christ... having no hope and without God in the world. But now in Christ Jesus you who once were far off have been brought near by the blood of Christ. (Ephesians 2:11-13)

God cared about you when He saw that you were without what?

_____

What kind of person cares about you when you have no hope?

_____

What did Jesus' blood accomplish?

_____

Jesus Takes the Pain

Then the high priest tore his clothes and said, "He has spoken blasphemy! Why do we need any more witnesses? Look, now you have heard the blasphemy. What do you think?" "He is worthy of death," they answered. Then they **spit** in his face and **struck** him with their fists. Others **slapped** him and said, "Prophesy to us, Messiah. Who hit you?"

When Pilate saw that he was getting nowhere, but that instead an uproar was starting, he took water and washed his hands in front of the crowd. "I am innocent of this man's blood," he said. "It is your responsibility!" All the people answered, "His blood is on us and on our children!" Then he released Barabbas to them. But he had Jesus **flogged**, and handed him over to be crucified...
Then the governor's soldiers took Jesus into the Praetorium and gathered the whole company of soldiers around him. They **stripped** him and put a scarlet robe on him, and then twisted together a crown of **thorns** and set it on his head. They put a staff in his right hand. Then they knelt in front of him and **mocked** him. "Hail, king of the Jews!" they said. They **spit** on him, and took the staff and **struck** him on the head again and again. After they had mocked him, they took off the robe and put his own clothes on him. Then they led him away to **crucify** him.

As they were going out, they met a man from Cyrene named Simon, and they forced him to [help] **carry** the cross. They came to a place called Golgotha (which means "the place of the skull"). There they offered Jesus wine to drink mixed with **gall**; but after tasting it, he refused to drink it. When they had crucified him, they divided up his clothes by casting lots. And sitting down, they kept watch over him there. Above his head they placed the written charge against him: THIS IS JESUS, THE KING OF THE JEWS.

Two rebels were crucified with him, one on his right and one on his left. Those who passed by hurled **insults** at him, shaking their heads and saying, "You who are going to destroy the temple and build it in three days, save yourself! Come down from the cross, if you are the Son of God!" In the same way the chief priests, the teachers of the law and the elders **mocked** him. "He saved others," they said, "but he can't save himself! He's the king of Israel! Let him come down now from the cross, and we will believe in him. He trusts in God. Let God rescue him now if he wants him, for he said, 'I am the Son of God.'" In the same way the rebels who were crucified with him also heaped insults on him.

From noon until three in the afternoon **darkness** came over all the land. About three in the afternoon **Jesus cried out** in a loud voice, "Eli, Eli, lema sabachthani?" (which means "My God, my God, why have you forsaken me?"). When some of those standing there heard this, they said, "He's calling Elijah." Immediately one of them ran and got a sponge. He filled it with wine **vinegar**, put it on a staff, and offered it to Jesus to drink. The rest said, "Now leave him alone. Let's see if Elijah comes to save him." And when Jesus had **cried out again** in a loud voice, he **gave up** his spirit.

At that moment the curtain of the temple was torn in two from top to bottom. The earth shook, the rocks split and the tombs broke open. The bodies of many holy people who had died were raised to life. They came out of the tombs after Jesus' resurrection and went into the holy city and appeared to many people. When the centurion and those with him who were guarding Jesus saw the earthquake and all that had happened, they were terrified, and exclaimed, "Surely he was the Son of God!" (Matthew 26:65-68, 27:24-54)

Have you ever suffered because you or someone else did something wrong? What did that look like? Feel like?

_____

_____

_____

The Cross was Jesus suffering *with* you, through the things that come against you in this world. How does it make you feel to know that God Himself identifies and suffers with you, in this life?

_____

_____

The Cross was also Jesus suffering *for* you, or *in place* of you. How does it make you feel to know that you will not face the ultimately consequences of sin? That God has saved you from that?

_____

_____

What kind of sacrifice did Jesus demonstrate was necessary to cover our sin? Was it quick and simple, or lengthy and painful?

_____

What kinds of things did He endure to demonstrate how far He was willing to go, to get you back?

_____

_____

_____

Does Jesus identify with your pain?

_____

The Meaning of the Cross

> And now He has made all of this plain to us by the appearing of Christ Jesus, our Savior. He broke the power of death and illuminated the way to life and immortality through the Good News. (2 Timothy 1:10)

What did Jesus' sacrifice obtain for you?

_____

Before He did that, what had power over you?

_____

> Day after day every priest stands and performs his religious duties; again and again he offers the same sacrifice, which can never take away sins. But when this Priest had offered for all time one sacrifice for sins, He sat down at the right hand of God, and since that time He waits for His enemies to be made His footstool. For by one sacrifice He has made perfect forever those who are being made holy...Then he adds: "Their sins and lawless acts I will remember no more." And

where these have been forgiven, sacrifice for sin is no longer necessary. (Hebrews 10:11-18)

Can earthly sacrifices earn forgiveness for sin?

_____

If sacrifices can't earn forgiveness, what about the personal sacrifices you make?

_____

What about all the good works you do in life? Can those earn you heaven?

_____

What wouldn't be fair about the ability to "earn" heaven by good works?

_____

_____

Why did Jesus' sacrifice end all sacrificial systems, for all time?

_____

_____

What did His sacrifice do for those who would follow Him?

_____

_____

How does God feel towards your sins now?

_____

It is impossible for the blood of bulls and goats to take away sins. Therefore, when Christ came into the world, He said: "Sacrifice and offering you did not desire, but a body you prepared for me; with burnt offerings and sin offerings you were not pleased. Then I said, Here I am—it is written about me in the scroll—I have come to do your will, my God." (Hebrews 10:4-7)

Did Jesus know what He was going to do before He came to earth?

_____

Did that stop Him from wanting to save you from sin?

_____

> For this reason the Father loves Me, because I lay down My life so that I may take it up again. No one has taken it away from Me, but I lay it down on My own initiative. I have authority to lay it down, and I have authority to take it up again. This commandment I received from My Father. (John 10:17-18)

Did Jesus have a choice to accept the Cross?

_____

If Jesus hadn't suffered, who would have had to do it?

_____

How does Jesus' death on the Cross show His love for you?

_____

_____

> For the joy set before Him, He endured the Cross, scorning its shame, and sat down at the right hand of the throne of God. (Hebrews 12:2)

How did Jesus feel about sacrificing Himself for you?

_____

Where does He sit now, advocating for you?

_____

> For He Himself is our peace, who has made us both one and has broken down in His flesh the dividing wall of hostility, by abolishing in His flesh the enmity, which is the Law of commandments contained in ordinances so that He might create in Himself one new man in place of the two, thus establishing peace, and might reconcile us both to God in one body through the Cross, thereby killing the hostility. (Ephesians 2:14-16)

The punishment Jesus received at the Cross ended what?

_____

_____

Does God accept you? Why?

_____

_____

What should you tell yourself when you feel like God might be punishing you, or that you are not doing good enough?

_____

_____

For God so loved the world that he gave his one and only Son, that whoever believes in him shall not perish but have eternal life. For God did not send his Son into the world to condemn the world, but to save the world through him. (John 3:16-17)

Explain in your own words what Jesus did for you on the Cross.

_____

_____

_____

_____

THE HOLY SPIRIT

Who is the Holy Spirit?

On one occasion, while [Jesus] was eating with [His disciples], he gave them this command: "Do not leave Jerusalem, but wait for the gift my Father promised, which you have heard me speak about. For John baptized with water, but in a few days you will be baptized with the Holy Spirit... you will receive power when the Holy Spirit comes on you; and you will be my witnesses in Jerusalem, and in all Judea and Samaria, and to the ends of the earth.   (Acts 1:4-8)

And behold, I am sending the promise of my Father upon you. But stay in the city until you are clothed with power from on high. (Luke 24:49)

Who sent the Holy Spirit?

_____

What was the Holy Spirit supposed to bring, when He came?

_____

What were they supposed to do after He came?

_____

I [John the Baptist] baptize you with water for repentance, but He who is coming after me is mightier than I, whose sandals I am not worthy to carry. He will baptize you with the Holy Spirit and fire. (Matthew 3:11)

What did John the Baptist promise that Jesus would do?

_____

If you then, who are evil, know how to give good gifts to your children, how much more will the heavenly Father give the Holy Spirit to those who ask him! (Luke 11:13)

Is the Holy Spirit a good gift to believers?

_____

Who does the Father give the Holy Spirit to?

_____

What does the Holy Spirit do?

And I will ask the Father, and he will give you another Helper, to be with you forever... (John 14:16)

What does the Holy Spirit do for you?

_____

_____

When the Spirit of truth comes, he will guide you into all truth. (John 16:13)

Can your intellect alone discover truth? Who do you need to help you?

_____

_____

When they deliver you over, do not be anxious how you are to speak or what you are to say, for what you are to say will be given to you in that hour. For it is not you who speak, but the Spirit of your Father speaking through you. (Matthew 10:19-20)

If you get into a difficult situation, who will help you speak?

_____

Whose voice does the Holy Spirit reflect?

_____

The Spirit helps us in our weakness. We do not know what we ought to pray for, but the Spirit himself intercedes for us through groaning too deep for words. And he who searches our hearts knows the mind of the Spirit, because the Spirit intercedes for God's people in accordance with the will of God. (Rom. 8:26-27)

What does this verse say the Holy Spirit does for us?

_____

What if you don't know what to pray for, or what God's will is, when you pray?

_____

How much emotion do you imagine is involved in "groaning too deep for words"?

_____

List a way you could apply this model of Spirit-led prayer to your own prayer life.

_____

_____

Encountering the Holy Spirit

> In Him you also trusted, after you heard the word of truth, the gospel of your salvation; in whom also, having believed, you were sealed with the Holy Spirit of promise" (Ephesians 1:13)

What does the Holy Spirit do when you first believe?

_____

Does every believer have the Holy Spirit?

_____

> Do not get drunk on wine, which leads to debauchery. Instead, be filled with the Spirit. (Ephesians 5:13)

Even though the Ephesians had already been "sealed" by the Holy Spirit, what does Paul now tell them that they need?

_____

Why would he tell them to be filled with the Spirit when they already had the Holy Spirit?

_____

What effect do people expect to get from alcohol? What are they seeking?

_____

Do people normally seek this experience once, or over and over?

_____

Should we be seeking this experience once, or over and over?

_____

O God, You are my God. Earnestly I seek You; my soul thirsts for You.
My body yearns for You in a dry and weary land without water...
Because Your loving devotion is better than life... (Psalm 63:1-3)

As the deer pants for streams of water, so my soul longs after You, O God. My soul thirsts for God, the living God. When shall I come and appear in God's presence?... (Psalm 42:1-2)

How important is experiencing God's presence in our lives?

_____

_____

What is it that "thirsts" for God?

_____

_____

If we "thirst" for God in these ways, can we drink just a little bit? Just one time?

_____

_____

Come, all you who are thirsty, come to the waters; and you who have no money, come, buy and eat! Come, buy wine and milk without money and without cost. Why spend money on what is not bread, and your labor on what does not satisfy? Listen to me, and eat what is good, and you will delight in the richest of fare. Give ear and come to me; listen, that you may live. (Isaiah 55:1-3)

Jesus says "Come..." Where is He inviting us to?

_____

Does responding to Him cost money? What *does* it cost?

_____

_____

What do we have to forego, to make pursuing Him a priority? Is there anything you believe He is asking you to put aside or lessen your pursuit of?

_____

Why do you think He compares His words to food?

_____

_____

How deeply in you does He want His life and presence to go?

_____

_____

When the day of Pentecost came, they were all together in one place. Suddenly a sound like the blowing of a violent wind came from heaven and filled the whole house where they were sitting. They saw what seemed to be tongues of fire that separated and came to rest on each of them. **All of them were filled with the Holy Spirit** and began to speak in other tongues as the Spirit enabled them...

Amazed and perplexed, they asked one another, "What does this mean?" Some, however, made fun of them and said, "They have had too much wine." Then Peter stood up with the Eleven, raised his voice and addressed the crowd: "Fellow Jews and all of you who live in Jerusalem, let me explain this to you; listen carefully to what I say. These people are not drunk, as you suppose. It's only nine in the morning! No, this is what was spoken by the prophet Joel:

'In the last days, God says, I will pour out my Spirit on all people. Your sons and daughters will prophesy, your young men will see visions, your old men will dream dreams. Even on my servants, both men and women, **I will pour out my Spirit in those days**, and they will prophesy. I will show wonders in the heavens above and signs on the earth below, blood and fire and billows of smoke. The sun will be turned to darkness and the moon to blood before the coming of the great and glorious day of the Lord. And everyone who calls on the name of the Lord will be saved...'

"Therefore let all Israel be assured of this: God has made this Jesus, whom you crucified, both Lord and Messiah." When the people heard this, they were cut to the heart and said to Peter and the other apostles, "Brothers, what shall we do?"

Peter replied, "Repent and be baptized, every one of you, in the name of Jesus Christ for the forgiveness of your sins**. And you will receive the gift of the Holy Spirit**. The promise is for you and your children and for all who are far off—for all whom the Lord our God will call." With many other words he warned them; and he pleaded with them, "Save yourselves from this corrupt generation." Those who accepted his message were baptized, and about three thousand were added to their number that day. (Acts 2:1-40)

What happened when the Holy Spirit was first poured on believers?

_____

_____

Did everyone recognize that this was the power of God? What did those who didn't believe in it say?

_____

Just 40 days before, Peter had been too afraid to admit he was Jesus' disciple. Does he look afraid here? How did the Holy Spirit change him?

_____

_____

According to Peter and the prophet Joel, what kinds of signs accompany the pouring out of the Holy Spirit?

_____

When the listeners asked Peter what they should do, what did he tell them? What would be the result?

_____

_____

Whom did Peter say the Holy Spirit was for?

_____

Who is the Giver of this gift?

_____

Do you think people need the Holy Spirit today? Why?

_____

_____

So I tell you: Ask, and it will be given to you; seek, and you will find; knock, and the door will be opened to you. For everyone who asks receives; he who seeks finds; and to him who knocks, the door will be opened. What father among you, if his son asks for a fish, will give him a snake instead? Or if he asks for an egg, will give him a scorpion? So if you who are evil know how to give good gifts to your children, how much more will your Father in heaven give the Holy Spirit to those who ask Him!" (Luke 11:9-13)

If you ask God for a gift that is good, will He give it to you?

_____

What gift in particular does Jesus say we should ask for?

_____

If you ask to be filled with the Holy Spirit what can you expect?

_____

Gifts of the Spirit

But grace was given to each one of us according to the measure of Christ's gift. Therefore it says, "When he ascended on high He led a host of captives, and He gave gifts to men"... And He himself gave the apostles, the prophets, the evangelists, the shepherds and teachers, to equip the saints for the work of ministry, for the building up of the body of Christ. (Ephesians 4:7-11)

Who gave the church spiritual gifts?

_____

What is the purpose of spiritual gifts?

_____

What offices help the church administer its gifts?

_____

_____

We have different gifts, according to the grace given to each of us. If your gift is prophesying, then prophesy in accordance with your faith; if it is serving, then serve; if it is teaching, then teach; if it is to encourage, then give encouragement;

if it is giving, then give generously; if it is to lead, do it diligently; if it is to show mercy, do it cheerfully. (Romans 12:6-8)

Which of these gifts describe you?

_____

_____

What would a church be like if its people were full of these gifts?

_____

Now to each one the manifestation of the Spirit is given for the common good... (1 Corinithians 12:7)

What is the purpose of the Holy Spirit's presence in church?

_____

Does everyone have a spiritual gift?

_____

Is it publicly visible?

_____

To one there is given through the Spirit a message of wisdom, to another a message of knowledge by means of the same Spirit, to another faith by the same Spirit, to another gifts of healing by that one Spirit, to another miraculous powers, to another prophecy, to another distinguishing between spirits, to another speaking in different kinds of tongues, and to still another the interpretation of tongues. All these are the work of one and the same Spirit, and He distributes them to each one, just as He determines... (1 Corinthians 12:8-:11)

Each gift expresses one quality of the complete love of God, and of the community He wants to build. Why don't we all have the same experiences in the Holy Spirit?

_____

_____

God has placed in the church first of all apostles, second prophets, third teachers, then miracles, then gifts of healing, of helping, of guidance, and of different kinds of tongues. (1 Corinthians 12:28)

Does God expect the church to be a miraculous Body?

_____

Speaking the truth in love, we are to grow up in every way into Him who is the head, into Christ, from whom the whole Body, joined and held together by every joint with which it is equipped, when each part is working properly, makes the Body grow so that it builds itself up in love. (Ephesians 4:15-16)

Is the Holy Spirit's intention to make us strange or off-putting? What should always be the motivating force behind operating in spiritual gifts?

_____

_____

Are some gifts more valuable than others?

_____

_____

What happens when all God's gifts are working together, in concert and in humility with one another?

_____

_____

Now about the gifts of the Spirit, brothers and sisters, I do not want you to be uninformed... There are different kinds of gifts, but the same Spirit distributes them. There are different kinds of service, but the same Lord. There are different kinds of working, but in all of them and in everyone it is the same God at work. (1 Corinthians 12:1, 4-6)

What does this passage say that spiritual gifts are for?

_____

_____

Are gifts meant to be divisive? Or in competition with one another?

Whose will is supposed to be operating behind all the gifts?

_____

Now eagerly desire the greater gifts... (1 Corinthians 12:31)
Follow the way of love and pursue gifts of the Spirit... (1 Corinthians 14:1)

Can you ask God for more spiritual gifts?

_____

Can you acquire more of them, or a greater measure of one?

_____

Does God want you to pursue them? Why? To promote what?

_____

Walking by the Spirit

So I say, walk by the Spirit, and you will not gratify the desires of the flesh. For the flesh desires what is contrary to the Spirit, and the Spirit what is contrary to the flesh. They are in conflict with each other, so that you are not to do what you want... (Galatians 5:16-17)

According to the Bible, what two forces are going on within a person?

_____

_____

_____

Now the acts of the flesh are obvious: sexual immorality, impurity and debauchery; idolatry and witchcraft; hatred, discord, jealousy, fits of rage, selfish ambition, dissensions, factions and envy; drunkenness, orgies, and the like. I warn you, as I did before, that those who live like this will not inherit the kingdom of God. But the fruit of the Spirit is love, joy, peace, forbearance, kindness, goodness, faithfulness, gentleness and self-control. (Gal. 5:18-22)

What two kinds of fruit do people produce?

Why would God compare the evidence of the Holy Spirit to fruit?

_____

_____

Which set of fruit are you producing more of?

_____

How can you tell if you are operating in the Holy Spirit correctly?

_____

_____

Those who belong to Christ Jesus have crucified the flesh with its passions and desires. Since we live by the Spirit, let us keep in step with the Spirit. (Galatians 5:24-25)

How do we produce more of the good fruit we want?

_____

_____

What does it mean to be led by the Holy Spirit?

_____

_____

Abide in me, as I abide in you. No branch can bear fruit by itself; it must remain in the vine. Neither can you bear fruit unless you remain in me. (John 15:4).

What must we always do, to bear spiritual fruit?

_____

_____

THE BIBLE

Building Your Foundation

All Scripture is God-breathed and is useful for teaching, rebuking, correcting and training in righteousness, so that the servant of God may be thoroughly equipped for every good work. (2 Timothy 3:16-17)

Is the Bible made up by men?

_____

How much of the Bible is inspired by God? Are there books or stories we can cut out? Why not?

_____

_____

What kinds of things is the Bible useful for?

_____

_____

What is the point of reading your Bible?

_____

For prophecy never had its origin in the human will, but prophets, though human, spoke from God as they were carried along by the Holy Spirit.
(2 Peter 1:21)

Who wrote the Bible?

_____

Who was behind this?

_____

Timothy, guard what has been entrusted to your care. Turn away from godless chatter and the opposing ideas of what is falsely called knowledge, which some have professed and thus gone astray from the faith. (1 Timothy 6:20-21).

What rivals your Bible as the source of knowledge and truth?

_____

What happens if you listen to these other sources of knowledge?

_____

"For My thoughts are not your thoughts, Nor are your ways My ways," declares the LORD. "For as the heavens are higher than the earth, so are My ways higher than your ways, And My thoughts than your thoughts. (Isaiah 55:8-9)

Do we naturally think like God?

_____

Trust in the LORD with all your heart and do not lean on your own understanding. In all your ways acknowledge Him, and He will make your pathways straight. (Proverbs 3:5-6)

What does God say we should do instead of relying on human wisdom?

_____

_____

What will result when we rely on God's wisdom?

_____

_____

Watch your life and doctrine closely. Pay close attention to yourself and to your teaching; persevere in these things, for as you do this you will ensure salvation both for yourself and for those who hear you. (1 Timothy 4:15-16)

How important is it, to pay attention to what you believe?

_____

For everything that was written in the past was written to teach us, so that through the endurance taught in the Scriptures, and the encouragement they provide, we might have hope. (Romans 15:4)

A lot of the Bible is history and stories. Why is it relevant to us today?

_____

_____

The lives of many people in the Bible were very hard. How is this supposed to help you when your life is hard?

_____

_____

> Now these things happened to them as an example, but they were written down for our instruction, on whom the end of the ages has come.   (1 Corinthians 10:11)

Where are we supposed to get our models of right and wrong ways to live and believe?

_____

Meditating on the Scriptures

> For the Word of God is alive and active. Sharper than any double-edged sword, it penetrates even to dividing soul and spirit, joints and marrow; it judges the thoughts and attitudes of the heart. And there is no creature hidden from His sight, but all things are open and laid bare to the eyes of Him. (Heb. 4:12-13)

How is Scripture different from every other kind of writing?

_____

_____

What effect does allowing God's Word into your heart have?

_____

_____

If lies or sins are hiding in your life or beliefs, what effect will God's Word have on them?

_____

Keep this Book of the Law always on your lips; meditate on it day and night, so that you may be careful to do everything written in it. Then you will be prosperous and successful. (Joshua 1:8)

What leads to prosperity and success?

_____

_____

What is the difference between reading and meditating?

_____

_____

Bind them on your heart always; tie them around your neck. When you walk, they will lead you; when you lie down, they will watch over you; and when you awake, they will talk with you. For the commandment is a lamp and the teaching a light, and the reproofs of discipline are the way of life. (Proverbs 6:21-23)

How does Scripture describe "meditating" on it?

_____

_____

How often are you supposed to consider what Scripture teaches?

_____

How can the words of Scripture "watch over" your life?

_____

_____

As a result, we are no longer to be children, tossed here and there by waves and carried about by every wind of doctrine, by the trickery of men, by craftiness in deceitful scheming. (Ephesians 4:14)

After we become established in the principles of Scripture, what are we able to avoid?

_____

Oh, how I love your law! I meditate on it all day long. Your commands are always with me and make me wiser than my enemies. I have more insight than all my teachers, for I meditate on your statutes. I have more understanding than the elders, for I obey your precepts. I have kept my feet from every evil path so that I might obey your word. I have not departed from your laws, for you yourself have taught me. How sweet are your words to my taste, sweeter than honey to my mouth! I gain understanding from your precepts; therefore I hate every wrong path. Your word is a lamp for my feet, and a light on my path. (Psalm 119:97-105)

How wise can you become if you meditate on Scripture?

_____

If you meditate on Scripture when you have difficult life choices, how will you receive guidance?

_____

_____

What is the result of diligent study and obedience to the Word of God?

_____

_____

Wisely Handling the Scripture

You study the Scriptures diligently because you think that in them you have eternal life. These are the very Scriptures that testify about Me. (John 5:29)

Can reading your Bible qualify you for heaven?

_____

What is the real purpose of the Word?

_____

Get rid of all moral filth and the evil that is so prevalent among you, and humbly accept the Word God has planted in your hearts, for it has the power to save your souls. But be doers of the Word, and not hearers only, deceiving yourselves. For anyone who listens to the Word but does not do what it says is like a man who looks intently at his face in a mirror, and after looking at himself, goes away and immediately forgets what he looks like.

But the one who looks into the perfect law, the law of liberty, and perseveres in it—not forgetting what they have heard but doing it—he will be blessed in what he does. If anyone thinks he is religious and does not bridle his tongue but deceives his heart, this person's religion is worthless. Religion that is pure and undefiled before God the Father, is this: to visit orphans and widows in their affliction, and to keep oneself unstained from the world. (James 1:21-27)

Does James believe in the importance of reading the Word?

_____

Why do you think James compares the Bible to a "mirror" that shows a man what he looks like?

_____

_____

_____

What is supposed to be the goal of reading Scripture and learning what it says?

_____

_____

Can reading the Bible magically change you into something you are not? What is required to authentically change?

_____

What kinds of things does James list as the main activities of healthy believers?

_____

_____

_____

What does James suggest the concern would be in putting intense hours of Bible study above all other ways of relating to God?

_____

_____

They arranged to meet Paul on a certain day, and came in even larger numbers to the place where he was staying. He witnessed to them from morning till evening, explaining about the kingdom of God, and from the Law of Moses and from the Prophets he tried to persuade them about Jesus. Some were convinced by what he said, but others would not believe.

They disagreed among themselves and began to leave after Paul had made this final statement: "The Holy Spirit rightly spoke through Isaiah the prophet to your fathers, saying, 'Go to this people and say, "You will keep on hearing, but will not understand; and you will keep on seeing but will not perceive; for the heart of this people has become dull, and with their ears they scarcely hear, and they have closed their eyes; otherwise they might see with their eyes and hear with their ears, and understand with their heart and return, and I would heal them." (Acts 28:25-27)

Can reading the Bible (or proclaiming its truths publicly) force people into salvation?

_____

Can we assume people just need to read the Bible, and then they will believe like we do?

_____

What do people need in order to understand and believe the Bible?

_____

What must come first?

_____

Now that same day two [disciples] were going to a village called Emmaus, about seven miles from Jerusalem. They were talking with each other about everything that had happened. As they talked and discussed these things with each other, Jesus Himself came up and walked along with them; but they were kept from recognizing him. He asked them, "What are you discussing together as you walk along?..."

...He said to them, "How foolish you are, and how slow to believe all that the prophets have spoken! Did not the Messiah have to suffer these things and then enter his glory?" And beginning with Moses and all the Prophets, He explained to them what was said in all the Scriptures concerning Himself. When He was at the table with them, He took bread, gave thanks, broke it and began to give it to them.

Then their eyes were opened and they recognized Him, and He disappeared from their sight. They asked each other, "Were not our hearts burning within us while He talked with us on the road and opened the Scriptures to us?" (Luke 24:13-17, 25-32)

Two believers walking on a road were talking about Christian ideas. Jesus was there, but were they connected to Jesus as they talked about them?

_____

Are you necessarily connected to Jesus because you are having Christian conversations?

_____

Does Jesus want to be connected to your thoughts and discussions?

_____

What do you have to do, to have Him enter in?

_____

Do we automatically understand the Bible, even if we've read it and studied it at length?

_____

What is the key theme of Scripture?

_____

Who has to open our eyes and explain it to us?

_____

How are we supposed to feel when the Spirit is moving through us and helping us to interpret/apply Scripture correctly?

_____

_____

PART II:
OBEYING GOD

HONORING ONE ANOTHER

The Ten Commandments

1. You shall have no other gods before me.

2. You shall not make for yourself an idol in the form of anything in heaven above or on the earth beneath, or in the waters below...

3. You shall not misuse the name of the Lord your God, for the Lord will not hold anyone guiltless who misuses his name.

4. Remember the Sabbath day by keeping it holy.

Honor your father and mother, so that you may live long in the land the Lord your 5. God is giving you.

6. You shall not murder.

7. You shall not commit adultery.

8. You shall not steal.

9. You shall not give false testimony against your neighbor.

10. You shall not covet your neighbor's house or his wife, his manservant or maidservant, his ox or donkey, or anything that belongs to your neighbor. (Exodus 20:3-17)

Which commandments address your relationships with other people?

_____

Honoring Your Parents

Children, obey your parents in the Lord, for this is right. "Honor your father and mother"—which is the first commandment with a promise— "so that it may go well with you and that you may enjoy long life on the earth." (Ephesians 6:2).

Why do you think honoring your parents comes first in the list of Commandments about relating well to others?

_____

_____

According to this verse, why is it important to honor your parents?

_____

_____

How might dishonoring your parents have a negative impact on your life?

_____

_____

How might having your parents' blessing add to your life?

_____

_____

The Lord disciplines those he loves, and he punishes everyone he accepts as a son. Endure hardship as discipline; God is treating you as sons. For what son is not disciplined by his father? If you are not disciplined (and everyone undergoes discipline), then you are illegitimate children and not true sons.

Moreover, we have all had human fathers who disciplined us and we respected them for it. How much more should we submit to the Father of our spirits and live! Our fathers disciplined us for a little while as they thought best; but God disciplines us for our good, that we may share in his holiness. No discipline seems pleasant at the time, but painful. Later on, however, it produces a harvest of righteousness and peace for those who have been trained by it. (Heb. 12:6-11)

Many people struggle with the discipline they received from their parents. What is one of the main roles of an earthly father?

_____

_____

How does the Bible say we should view this role?

_____

_____

How do most people respond to those who play this role in their lives?

_____

_____

Is discipline from an earthly parent perfect? Does God know that?

_____

_____

What does this verse imply about parents who are negligent or too permissive?

_____

> Which of you, if his son asks for bread, will give him a stone? Or if he asks for a fish, will give him a snake? If you, then, though you are evil, know how to give good gifts to your children, how much more will your Father in heaven give good gifts to those who ask him! (Matthew 7:9-11)

To what earthly role does God choose to compare Himself to?

_____

This passage assumes you have a good father, not an evil one. Name some ways that God is like a good father.

_____

_____

_____

If you dishonor a good mother and father here on earth, you are also dishonoring their role, which means you are dishonoring who?

_____

_____

Are there any ways you have dishonored your parents that you should repent of? Or ask forgiveness for? (If this is a complicated issue for you, consider seeking a mentor who can counsel you through to freedom.)

_____

_____

Honoring Authority

Let everyone be subject to the governing authorities, for there is no authority except that which God has established. The authorities that exist have been established by God. Consequently, whoever rebels against the authority is rebelling against what God has instituted, and those who do so will bring judgment on themselves. For rulers hold no terror for those who do right, but for those who do wrong.

Do you want to be free from fear of the one in authority? Then do what is right and you will be commended. For the one in authority is God's servant for your good. But if you do wrong, be afraid, for rulers do not bear the sword for no reason. They are God's servants, agents of wrath to bring punishment on the wrongdoer.

Therefore, it is necessary to submit to the authorities, not only because of possible punishment but also as a matter of conscience. This is also why you pay taxes. The authorities are God's servants who devote themselves to their work. (Romans 13:1-5)

Where did the idea of earthly authorities come from?

_____

How does God tell you to feel free while under the power that authorities have?

_____

_____

What main power do authorities wield?

_____

Does God indicate that this power is right or wrong?

_____

What two things does God say rebelling against authority brings?

_____

_____

Rome was the pagan nation that crucified Jesus and persecuted His followers. Do you think they were always right, or easy to submit to?

_____

In what way was an evil empire like Rome part of God's system, or "God's servant for their good"?

_____

_____

What kind of attitude does this passage indicate we should have towards our government, police, employers, etc.? Even though they aren't perfect?

_____

_____

What blessings will that bring to your life?

_____

_____

> Pay everyone what you owe him: taxes to whom taxes are due, revenue to whom revenue is due, respect to whom respect is due, honor to whom honor is due. (Romans 13:6-7)

What kind of attitude towards societal order does the Bible ask us to have?

_____

What kind of society would we create if we did not have this attitude? If we felt and behaved the opposite?

_____

What kind of witness would that be, to the world at large?

_____

_____

Can you see any other fallout from being stingy about giving respect and honor?

_____

_____

> Previously, you let yourselves be slaves to impurity and lawlessness, which led ever deeper into sin. Now you must give yourselves to be slaves to righteous living so that you will become holy. (Romans 6:19)

> ...Indeed, sin is lawlessness (1 John 3:4)

Does a slave love doing what they must do?

_____

What was the problem when we lived for ourselves, as lawbreakers?

_____

_____

If the devil is the author of sin, who is the author of lawlessness or rebellious behavior?

_____

What does the world see, when you train yourself to live righteously?

_____

_____

Honoring Your Community

> Obey your leaders and submit to them, for they watch over your souls as those who must give an account. To this end, allow them to lead with joy and not with grief, for that would be of no advantage to you. (Hebrews 13:17)

This Scripture is written about church leadership. Have you ever had to lead or pastor anyone before? What did you hope from your followers?

_____

_____

What important thing does God hold church leaders accountable for?

_____

Does God have mercy on leaders because of that task?

_____

What are some ways you can show mercy towards your leaders?

_____

_____

_____

_____

> I am afraid that when I come, I may not find you as I wish, and you may not find me as you wish. I fear that there may be quarreling, jealousy, rage, rivalry, slander, gossip, arrogance, and disorder. (2 Corinthians 12:20)

What was Paul worried about, in the Greek church?

_____

_____

Do you see these things in churches today? Name a few ways they can manifest.

_____

_____

How does a culture that encourages dishonor enable these things?

_____

_____

> The acts of the flesh are obvious: sexual immorality, impurity, and debauchery; idolatry and sorcery; hatred, discord, jealousy, and rage; rivalries, divisions, factions, and envy; drunkenness, orgies, and the like. I warn you, as I did before, that those who practice such things will not inherit the kingdom of God. (Galatians 5:20-21)

Where does quarreling, rivalry, anger, divisiveness, and competitiveness come from?

_____

Why should these not typify our churches?

_____

_____

How can a culture of honor work against these things?

_____

_____

"If you forgive men their trespasses, your heavenly Father will also forgive you." (Matthew 6:14)

Parents, authorities, and people in the church hurt us. Should we hold it against them, especially if they knew better or did it intentionally? Why?

_____

_____

How does forgiveness witness Jesus' character?

_____

_____

How does forgiveness change a culture?

_____

_____

_____

"Father, forgive them, for they know not what they do." (Luke 23:34)

Do you always know when you have hurt someone? Why might you *not* know?

_____

Do you always know if you are putting off someone you're leading or coaching? In this situation, why might you not know?

_____

_____

When you have hurt people in the past, about what percentage of the time was it intentional?

_____

In your life, many people have forgiven you for many things. What is the benefit to you, from that covering?

_____

_____

Can you extend that benefit to others?

_____

PURITY

The Ten Commandments

1. You shall have no other gods before me.

2. You shall not make for yourself an idol in the form of anything in heaven above or on the earth beneath, or in the waters below...

3. You shall not misuse the name of the Lord your God, for the Lord will not hold anyone guiltless who misuses his name.

4. Remember the Sabbath day by keeping it holy.

Honor your father and mother, so that you may live long in the land the Lord your 5. God is giving you.

6. You shall not murder.

7. You shall not commit adultery.

8. You shall not steal.

9. You shall not give false testimony against your neighbor.

10. You shall not covet your neighbor's house or his wife, his manservant or maidservant, his ox or donkey, or anything that belongs to your neighbor. (Exodus 20:3-17)

Which two commandments deal with sexual desire outside marriage?

_____

What is the 10th commandment saying about moral purity?

_____

> But I tell you that anyone who looks at a woman lustfully has already committed adultery with her in his heart...(Matthew 5:28)

According to Jesus, is it enough to simply not have sexual intercourse outside of marriage? Why?

_____

_____

What part of you is the source of lust?

_____

What part of you is Jesus most concerned about?

_____

Based on this, would Jesus be concerned about women having lustful thoughts too?

_____

What things in your sphere most encourage lustful thoughts in your life?

_____

_____

_____

"If your right eye causes you to sin, gouge it out and throw it away. It is better for you to lose one part of your body than for your whole body to be thrown into hell. And if your right hand causes you to sin, cut it off and throw it away. It is better for you to lose one part of your body than for your whole body to go into hell." (Matthew 5:29-30)

Where does Jesus say people may end up if they do not deal with lust?

_____

Why does Jesus spotlight the gateways of sight and touch here?

_____

_____

How aggressive should you be, to get lust out of your life?

_____

_____

Why God Cares

I saw the holy city, the new Jerusalem, coming down out of heaven from God, prepared as a bride adorned for her husband... Then one of the seven angels with the seven bowls full of the seven last plagues came and said to me, "Come, I will show you the bride, the wife of the Lamb." (Revelation 22:2, 9)

What will happen to the Church at the End of time?

_____

_____

Why is marriage a good analogy for the Church's future partnership with Christ?

_____

_____

I am jealous for you with a godly jealousy. For I promised you to one husband, to present you as a pure virgin to Christ. I am afraid, however, that just as Eve was deceived by the serpent's cunning, your minds may be led astray from simple and pure devotion to Christ. (2 Corinthians 11:2-3)

Why does the Bible connect Eve's deception by Satan, and leading astray, to adultery? What did she turn to? Whom did she abandon?

_____

_____

_____

How do you remain a "virgin" to Christ?

_____

_____

Flee from sexual immorality. Every other sin a man can commit is outside his body, but he who sins sexually sins against his own body. Do you not know that your body is a temple of the Holy Spirit who is in you, whom you have received from God? You are not your own; you were bought at a price. Therefore, glorify God with your body. (1 Corinthians 6:18-20)

As a believer, who is living inside you?

_____

Why would sexual immorality threaten this, or adulterate this?

_____

_____

How did Jesus purchase your body?

_____

_____

_____

How are you supposed to live now, in light of that fact?

_____

_____

> For you must not worship any other god, for the LORD, whose name is Jealous, is a jealous God. (Exodus 34:14)

Why does God use the word "jealous" to describe His feelings towards us?

_____

_____

_____

How can we show Him that we are devoted to Him, as a bride to our Bridegroom?

_____

_____

> But among you, as is proper among the saints, there must not be even a hint of sexual immorality, or of any kind of impurity, or of greed. Nor should there be obscenity, foolish talk, or crude joking, which are out of character, but rather thanksgiving. For of this you can be sure: No immoral, impure, or greedy person (that is, an idolater), has any inheritance in the kingdom of Christ and of God. (Ephesians 3:3-6)

What is God's standard for purity?

_____

_____

What kinds of other behaviors go with sexual indecency or debasement? How do those who are sexually debased talk?

_____

_____

What are you idolizing if you live a lifestyle of impurity or immorality?

_____

_____

Let no one deceive you with empty words, for because of such things God's wrath comes on the sons of disobedience. Therefore do not be partakers with them. For you were once darkness, but now you are light in the Lord. Walk as children of light, for the fruit of the light consists in all goodness, righteousness, and truth. Have no fellowship with the fruitless deeds of darkness, but rather expose them. For it is shameful even to mention what the disobedient do in secret. (Ephesians 5:7-12)

How can friends or society encourage you to lower your sexual standards?

_____

_____

_____

Should you believe these voices?

_____

Is most sexual immorality done in secret? The darkness? Why?

_____

_____

What should you do, to walk as a child of the light?

_____

The Trap of Lust (2 Samuel 11:3-12:12)

One evening David got up from his bed and walked around on the roof of the palace. From the roof he saw a woman bathing. The woman was very beautiful, and David sent someone to find out about her. The man said, "Isn't this Bathsheba, the daughter of Eliam and the wife of Uriah the Hittite?" Then David sent messengers to get her. She came to him, and he slept with her. (She had purified herself from her uncleanness.) Then she went back home. The woman conceived and sent word to David, saying, "I am pregnant."

When did David's sin begin?

_____

So David sent this word to Joab: "Send me Uriah the Hittite." And Joab sent him to David. When Uriah came to him, David asked him how Joab was, how the soldiers were and how the war was going. Then David said to Uriah, "Go down to your house and wash your feet." So Uriah left the palace, and a gift from the king was sent after him. But Uriah slept at the entrance to the palace with all his master's servants and did not go down to his house.

When David was told, "Uriah did not go home," he asked him, "Haven't you just come from a distance? Why didn't you go home?" Uriah said to David, "The ark and Israel and Judah are staying in tents, and my master Joab and my lord's men are camped in the open fields. How could I go to my house to eat and drink and lie with my wife? As surely as you live, I will not do such a thing!" Then David said to him, "Stay here one more day, and tomorrow I will send you back." So Uriah remained in Jerusalem that day and the next. At David's invitation, he ate and drank with him, and David made him drunk. But in the evening Uriah went out to sleep on his mat among his master's servants; he did not go home.

When Bathsheba got pregnant, how did David first try to cover it up?

_____

_____

In the morning David wrote a letter to Joab and sent it with Uriah. In it he wrote, "Put Uriah in the front line where the fighting is fiercest. Then withdraw from him so he will be struck down and die." So while Joab had the city under siege, he put Uriah at a place where he knew the strongest defenders were. When the men of the city came out and fought against Joab, some of the men in David's army fell; moreover, Uriah the Hittite died. When Uriah's wife heard that her husband was dead, she mourned for him. After the time of mourning was over, David had her brought to his house, and she became his wife and bore him a son. But the thing David had done displeased the LORD.

When that failed, what did David then do?

_____

_____

The LORD sent Nathan to David. When he came to him, he said, "There were two men in a certain town, one rich and the other poor. The rich man had a very large number of sheep and cattle, but the poor man had nothing except one little ewe lamb he had bought. He raised it, and it grew up with him and his children. It shared his food, drank from his cup and even slept in his arms. It was like a daughter to him. "Now a traveler came to the rich man, but the rich man refrained from taking one of his own sheep or cattle to prepare a meal for the traveler who had come to him. Instead, he took the ewe lamb that belonged to the poor man and prepared it for the one who had come to him."

David burned with anger against the man and said to Nathan, "As surely as the LORD lives, the man who did this deserves to die! He must pay for that lamb four times over, because he did such a thing and had no pity."

Then Nathan said to David, "You are the man! This is what the LORD, the God of Israel, says: 'I anointed you king over Israel, and I delivered you from the hand of Saul. I gave your master's house to you, and your master's wives into your arms. I gave you the house of Israel and Judah. And if all this had been too little, I would have given you even more. Why did you despise the word of the LORD by doing what is evil in his eyes? You struck down Uriah the Hittite with the sword and took his wife to be your own. You killed him with the sword of the Ammonites. Now, therefore, the sword will never depart from your house, because you despised me and took the wife of Uriah the Hittite to be your own. This is what the LORD says: 'Out of your own household I am going to bring calamity upon you. Before your very eyes I will take your wives and give them to one who is close to you, and he will lie with your wives in broad daylight. You did it in secret, but I will do this thing in broad daylight before all Israel."

The Lord loved David fiercely, but did this permit Him to overlook David's sin?

_____

How many/which of the Ten Commandments did David end up breaking?

_____

In what two ways did God punish David for his sin?

_____

_____

What would have happened if God had not loved David enough to bring in Nathan?

_____

What could have then happened to David?

_____

_____

Why is sin, especially lust, so dangerous?

_____

_____

Finding Freedom

Then Jesus straightened up and asked her [the woman caught in adultery], "Woman, where are your accusers? Has no one condemned you?" "No one, Lord," she answered. "Then neither do I condemn you," Jesus declared. "Now go and sin no more." (John 8:11)

How did God address the woman struggling in adultery?

_____

_____

What does Jesus ask you to do, to be free?

_____

_____

Then Peter came to Jesus and asked, "Lord, how many times shall I forgive my brother who sins against me? Up to seven times?" Jesus answered, "I tell you, not just seven times, but up to seventy times seven times! (Matthew 18:21-22)

How is lust a sin against another person?

_____

If people are supposed to forgive you, can God forgive you?

_____

How many times will He forgive you?

_____

> Do you not know that the wicked will not inherit the kingdom of God? Do not be deceived: Neither the sexually immoral, nor idolaters, nor adulterers, nor men who submit to or perform homosexual acts, nor thieves, nor the greedy, nor drunkards, nor verbal abusers, nor swindlers, will inherit the kingdom of God. And that is what some of you **were**. **But** you were washed, you were sanctified, you were justified, in the name of the Lord Jesus Christ and by the Spirit of our God. (1 Corinthians 6:9-11)

Is sexual sin worse than other kinds of sins?

_____

Are people who have committed sexual sins, even homosexual sins, disqualified from being saved?

_____

What has cleansed you?

_____

How are you to walk if you have struggled with lust or immorality?

_____

_____

> Husbands, love your wives, just as Christ loved the church and gave himself up for her to make her holy, cleansing her by the washing with water through the Word, and to present her to himself as a radiant church, without stain or wrinkle or any other blemish, but holy and blameless. (Ephesians 5:25-27)

The picture of earthly marriage here is one of cherishing and single-minded devotion. How does Jesus feel about you, as part of His bride?

_____

_____

How does Jesus clean His bride?

_____

What should you do, when you find yourself in need of cleansing?

_____

_____

How does Jesus see you, if you repent from the heart? What about your sins and stains?

_____

_____

INTEGRITY

The Ten Commandments

1. You shall have no other gods before me.

2. You shall not make for yourself an idol in the form of anything in heaven above or on the earth beneath, or in the waters below...

3. You shall not misuse the name of the Lord your God, for the Lord will not hold anyone guiltless who misuses his name.

4. Remember the Sabbath day by keeping it holy.

Honor your father and mother, so that you may live long in the land the Lord your 5. God is giving you.

6. You shall not murder.

7. You shall not commit adultery.

8. You shall not steal.

9. You shall not give false testimony against your neighbor.

10. You shall not covet your neighbor's house or his wife, his manservant or maidservant, his ox or donkey, or anything that belongs to your neighbor. (Exodus 20:3-17)

Which commandment deals with telling the truth?

_____

What does the commandment indicate is wrong with lying?

_____

Now a man named Ananias, together with his wife Sapphira, also sold a piece of property. With his wife's full knowledge he kept back part of the money for himself, but brought the rest and put it at the apostles' feet. Then Peter said, "Ananias, how is it that Satan has so filled your heart that you have lied to the Holy Spirit and have kept for yourself some of the money you received for the land? Didn't it belong to you before it was sold? And after it was sold, wasn't the money at your disposal? What made you think of doing such a thing? You have not lied to men but to God."

When Ananias heard this, he fell down and died. And great fear seized all who heard what had happened. Then the young men came forward, wrapped up his body, and carried him out and buried him. About three hours later his wife came

in, not knowing what had happened. Peter asked her, "Tell me, is this the price you and Ananias got for the land?" "Yes," she said, "that is the price." Peter said to her, "How could you agree to test the Spirit of the Lord? Look! The feet of the men who buried your husband are at the door, and they will carry you out also." At that moment she fell down at his feet and died. Then the young men came in and, finding her dead, carried her out and buried her beside her husband. Great fear seized the whole church and all who heard about these events.
(Acts 5:1-11)

What sin did Ananias and Sapphira commit?

_____

What sins did they commit first, which made them need to lie?

_____

_____

What did they want everyone in the early church to think, that was not correct?

_____

_____

How does sin corrupt people close to you?

_____

_____

What does God want us to know about willful sin?

_____

What point did God impress upon the first church, about honesty?

_____

_____

Do not swear by your head, for you cannot make even one hair white or black. Simply let your 'Yes' be 'Yes,' and your 'No,' 'No'; anything beyond this comes from the evil one. (Matthew 5:36-37)

Why do people "swear" or "promise" they will do something?

_____

_____

Why does God say not to do this?

_____

_____

To whom does God attribute the attitude of being vehement and wanting to take control of a situation?

_____

How does speaking simply relate to honesty?

_____

_____

How would this passage speak to exaggerating or hiding the truth?

_____

_____

> Then the man and his wife heard the voice of the LORD God walking in the garden in the breeze of the day, and they hid themselves from the presence of the LORD God among the trees of the garden. So the LORD God called out to the man, "Where are you?" "I heard Your voice in the garden," he replied, "and I was afraid because I was naked; so I hid myself." (Genesis 3:8-10)

How did Adam and Eve "lie" to God? What did their sin make them feel they needed to do?

_____

How is sin connected to dishonesty?

_____

To whom are we lying to?

_____

You belong to your father, the devil, and you want to carry out your father's desires. He was a murderer from the beginning, not holding to the truth, for there is no truth in him. When he lies, he speaks his native language, for he is a liar and the father of lies. (John 8:44)

If you tell lies, who are you acting like?

_____

God is not man, that he should lie, or a son of man, that he should change his mind. Has he said, and will he not do it? Or has he spoken, and will he not fulfill it? (Numbers 23:13)

Does God ever lie?

_____

If He promises something, will He do it?

_____

Why would God care that you knew He was honest?

_____

_____

Does God ask you to do things that He doesn't do Himself?

_____

Why does God want you to keep your word?

_____

CONTENTMENT

The Ten Commandments

1. You shall have no other gods before me.

2. You shall not make for yourself an idol in the form of anything in heaven above or on the earth beneath, or in the waters below...

3. You shall not misuse the name of the Lord your God, for the Lord will not hold anyone guiltless who misuses his name.

4. Remember the Sabbath day by keeping it holy.

Honor your father and mother, so that you may live long in the land the Lord your 5. God is giving you.

6. You shall not murder.

7. You shall not commit adultery.

8. You shall not steal.

9. You shall not give false testimony against your neighbor.

10. You shall not covet your neighbor's house or his wife, his manservant or maidservant, his ox or donkey, or anything that belongs to your neighbor. (Exodus 20:3-17)

Which two commandments deal with money?

_____

What heart attitude does the 10th Commandment deal with?

_____

How do these two commandments go together?

_____

_____

The Story of Judas

But one of his disciples, Judas Iscariot, who was later to betray him, objected, "Why wasn't this perfume sold and the money given to the poor? It was worth a year's wages." He did not say this because he cared about the poor but because he was a thief; as keeper of the money bag, he used to help himself to what was put into it. (John 12:4-6)

What sin did Judas have, even before he betrayed Jesus? What did he do?

_____

_____

What does this passage indicate is the relationship between loving money and caring about the fortune of others?

_____

_____

Then one of the Twelve-- the one called Judas Iscariot-- went to the chief priests and asked, "What are you willing to give me if I hand him over to you?" So they counted out for him thirty silver coins. From then on Judas watched for an opportunity to hand him over.   (Matthew 26:14-16)

How much was Judas' integrity worth, to himself?

_____

How much was Jesus worth, to Judas?

_____

Do you think Judas would have betrayed Jesus if there was no money involved?

_____

How were the Ten Commandments prophetic, regarding what would happen to Jesus? What did they name, which would affect His life and death?

_____

_____

Jesus was troubled in spirit and testified, "I tell you the truth, one of you is going to betray me." His disciples stared at one another, at a loss to know which of them he meant. One of them, the disciple whom Jesus loved, was reclining next to him. Simon Peter motioned to this disciple and said, "Ask him which one he means." Leaning back against Jesus, he asked him, "Lord, who is it?" Jesus answered, "It is the one to whom I will give this piece of bread when I have dipped it in the dish." Then, dipping the piece of bread, he gave it to Judas Iscariot, son of Simon.

As soon as Judas took the bread, Satan entered into him. "What you are about to do, do quickly," Jesus told him, but no one at the meal understood why Jesus said this to him. Since Judas had charge of the money, some thought Jesus was telling him to buy what was needed for the Feast, or to give something to the poor. As soon as Judas had taken the bread, he went out. And it was night. (John 13:21-30)

Did others notice the depth of Judas' greed, while he walked with Jesus? Who noticed?

_____

How does it make Jesus feel when He senses His followers are not in alignment with Him?

_____

Whom does God say Judas was under the influence of, when he negotiated this transaction?

_____

While he was still speaking, Judas, one of the Twelve, arrived. With him was a large crowd armed with swords and clubs, sent from the chief priests and the elders of the people. Now the betrayer had arranged a signal with them: "The one I kiss is the man; arrest him." Going at once to Jesus, Judas said, "Greetings, Rabbi!" and kissed him. (Matthew 26:47-49)

When Judas, who had betrayed him, saw that Jesus was condemned, he was seized with remorse and returned the thirty silver coins to the chief priests and the elders. "I have sinned," he said, "for I have betrayed innocent blood." "What is that to us?" they replied. "That's your responsibility." So Judas threw the money into the temple and left. Then he went away and hanged himself.
(Matthew 27:3-5)

How did Judas feel, after he had betrayed Jesus?

_____

_____

How did Judas see the money he had gained?

_____

_____

Why is the love of money so dangerous for us?

_____

_____

Judas was part of Jesus' ministry team. In what ways do ministers today betray their calling for money?

_____

_____

Can you think of any way that ministers use their position or the Bible to justify greed?

_____

_____

What will be the end of those who trade their ministry for money?

_____

_____

Is your integrity priceless, to you? How will you know?

_____

_____

The Story of the Sons of Eli

Eli's sons were wicked men; they had no regard for the LORD. It was the practice of the priests with the people that whenever anyone offered a sacrifice and while the meat was being boiled, the servant of the priest would come with a three-pronged fork in his hand. He would plunge it into the pan or kettle or caldron or pot, and the priest would take for himself whatever the fork brought up.

This is how they treated all the Israelites who came to Shiloh. But even before the fat was burned, the servant of the priest would come and say to the man who was sacrificing, "Give the priest some meat to roast; he won't accept boiled meat from you, but only raw." If the man said to him, "Let the fat be burned up first, and then take whatever you want," the servant would then answer, "No, hand it over now; if you don't, I'll take it by force." This sin of the young men was very great in the LORD's sight, for they were treating the LORD's offering with contempt... (1 Samuel 2:12-17)

What did Eli's sons do, that was so displeasing to God?

_____

_____

How did they use their position in ministry to gain financially?

_____

_____

...Now Eli, who was very old, heard about everything his sons were doing to all Israel and how they slept with the women who served at the entrance to the Tent of Meeting. So he said to them, "Why do you do such things? I hear from all the people about these wicked deeds of yours. No, my sons; it is not a good report that I hear spreading among the LORD's people. If a man sins against another man, God may mediate for him; but if a man sins against the LORD, who will intercede for him?" His sons, however, did not listen to their father's rebuke... (1 Samuel 2:22-25)

What other sin went with their abuse of power and money?

_____

Did other people know what was going on?

_____

Were they able to continue in ministry for some time, even though they were in sin?

_____

_____

...Now a man of God came to Eli and said to him, "... Why do you scorn my sacrifice and offering that I prescribed for my dwelling? Why do you honor your sons more than me by fattening yourselves on the choice parts of every offering made by my people Israel?" Therefore the LORD, the God of Israel, declares: 'I promised that your house and your father's house would minister before me forever.' But now the LORD declares: 'Far be it from me! Those who honor me I will honor, but those who despise me will be disdained. The time is coming when I will cut short your strength and the strength of your father's house, so that there will not be an old man in your family line and you will see distress in my dwelling. Although good will be done to Israel, in your family line there will never be an old man. Every one of you that I do not cut off from my altar will be spared only to blind your eyes with tears and to grieve your heart, and all your descendants will die in the prime of life. And what happens to your two sons, Hophni and Phinehas, will be a sign to you-- they will both die on the same day... (1 Samuel 2:27-34)

...The Israelites were defeated and every man fled to his tent. The slaughter was very great; Israel lost thirty thousand foot soldiers. The ark of God was captured, and Eli's two sons, Hophni and Phinehas, died. That same day a Benjamite ran from the battle line and went to Shiloh, his clothes torn and dust on his head. When he arrived, there was Eli sitting on his chair by the side of the road, watching, because his heart feared for the ark of God...

Eli asked, "What happened, my son?" The man who brought the news replied, "Israel fled before the Philistines, and the army has suffered heavy losses. Also your two sons, Hophni and Phinehas, are dead, and the ark of God has been captured." When he mentioned the ark of God, Eli fell backward off his chair by the side of the gate. His neck was broken and he died, for he was an old man and heavy. He had led Israel forty years. (1 Samuel 4:10-18)

When they were confronted and did not repent, what happened to Hophni and Phineas?

_____

_____

Were they the only ones affected by their sin? Who else was?

_____

_____

_____

Furthermore, select capable men from among the people— God-fearing, trustworthy men who are averse to dishonest gain. Appoint them over the people as leaders of thousands, of hundreds, of fifties, and of tens. (Exod. 18:21)

Why does God want his leaders to hate covetousness, or unjust gain?

_____

_____

Trusting God

But godliness with contentment is great gain. We have brought nothing into the world, so we cannot take anything out of it either. And if we have food and clothing, with these we shall be content.

But those who want to get rich fall into temptation and a snare and many foolish and harmful desires which plunge men into ruin and destruction. For the love of money is a root of all sorts of evil, and some by longing for it have wandered away from the faith, and pierced themselves with many pains.

But flee from these things, you man of God; and pursue righteousness, godliness, faith, love, perseverance and gentleness. Fight the good fight of faith; take hold of the eternal life to which you were called, and you made the good confession in the presence of many witnesses. (1 Timothy 6:6-12)

What is the root of all kinds of evil?

_____

What basic provisions does God say should give us contentment?

_____

What happens to those who begin to pursue money while in ministry?

_____

_____

What should you pursue instead of money?

_____

_____

I am not saying this out of need, for I have learned to be content regardless of my circumstances. I know how to live humbly, and I know how to abound. I am accustomed to any and every situation— to being filled and being hungry, to having plenty and having need. I can do all things through Christ who gives me strength. (Philippians 4:11-13)

Does Paul say we should avoid being poor?

_____

Does Paul say we should avoid being rich?

_____

Remember this: Whoever sows sparingly will also reap sparingly, and whoever sows generously will also reap generously. Each one should give what he has decided in his heart to give, not out of regret or compulsion. For God loves a cheerful giver. (2 Corinthians 9:6-7).

What does God want us to focus on, instead of loving money?

_____

What should always be the source of how much you decide to give?

_____

What is the key to offering an opportunity for people to give?

_____

_____

What is the benefit of giving generously?

_____

_____

Now He who supplies seed to the sower and bread for food will supply and multiply your store of seed and will increase the harvest of your righteousness. You will be enriched in every way to be generous on every occasion, and your giving through us will produce thanksgiving to God. (2 Corinthians 10:10-11)

Why don't you need to worry about giving sacrificially to something you believe in?

_____

_____

Is God's will for Christians to be poor? How do you know?

_____

_____

_____

WALKING IN FREEDOM

Receiving Forgiveness

We all stumble in many ways (James 3:2)

Does being a Christian make you perfect?

_____

If we claim to be without sin, we deceive ourselves and the truth is not in us. (1 John 1:8)

If you think you never sin or need forgiveness, what does this say?

_____

_____

If we confess our sins, He is faithful and just to forgive us our sins and purify us from all unrighteousness. (1 John 1:9)

If you sin, what should you do?

_____

_____

Will God forgive you?

_____

What will He also do?

_____

_____

How does it make you feel, to know that God will forgive you if you confess?

_____

I am writing this to you so that you will not sin. But if anyone does sin, we have an advocate who pleads our case before the Father. He is Jesus Christ, the one who is truly righteous. (1 John 2:1)

Is God's provision for sin a license to do it?

_____

Who will appear before the Father on your behalf when you repent from the heart?

_____

> As far as the east is from the west, so far has He removed our transgressions from us. (Psalm 103:12)

Do your stains stay? Where do they go?

_____

_____

Does God keep a record of your wrongs?

_____

Extending Forgiveness

> For if you forgive men when they sin against you, your heavenly Father will also forgive you. But if you do not forgive men their sins, your Father will not forgive your sins. (Matthew 6:14-15)

Should you keep a record of someone else's wrongs?

_____

What is the only thing God wants in return, for the kindness He shows you?

_____

_____

Is forgiveness your choice?

_____

Is there anyone you need to choose to forgive?

_____

_____

Are there reasons you cannot forgive them?

_____

_____

_____

What do you think Jesus would tell you in response?

_____

> Why do you look at the speck of sawdust in your brother's eye and pay no attention to the plank in your own eye? How can you say to your brother, 'Let me take the speck out of your eye,' when all the time there is a plank in your own eye? You hypocrite, first take the plank out of your own eye, and then you will see clearly to remove the speck from your brother's eye. (Matthew 7:3-5)

Do most people want to deal with our own faults first, or the faults of others first?

_____

Do most people tend to see their own faults as bigger or smaller than they really are?

_____

Do most people tend to see others' faults as bigger or smaller than they really are?

_____

When we examine others' faults, do we tend to see them accurately, or simpler than they really are? Sympathetically or unsympathetically?

_____

What does Jesus require us to do before we consider the faults of others?

_____

_____

What size does Jesus say our part of the problem really is?

_____

How long do you think it would take to remove a problem of that size?

_____

List several people in your life that you currently feel critical of, and why?

_____

_____

_____

Can you show the love of Jesus to these people? List a few ways that you could.

_____

_____

_____

Pray and ask Jesus if there are any logs in your own eye that He wants you to deal with before your remove the specks from the people you wrote down.

_____

_____

_____

Blessed are the merciful, for they will be shown mercy. (Matthew 5:7)

Judgment without mercy will be shown to anyone who has not been merciful. Mercy triumphs over judgment! (James 2:13)

Do you want God to treat you with mercy or judgment?

_____

How will God treat those who do not show mercy?

_____

For in the same way you judge others, you will be judged. With the measure you use, it will be measured to you. (Matthew 7:2)

If you are critical towards others, how will God be towards you?

_____

If you hold others to exceedingly high standards, what standards will God hold you to?

_____

If you forgive much, what will happen to you?

_____

_____

Can you accept God's unique rules about forgiveness, both receiving and extending?

_____

Based on this, can you formulate a wise way to treat people who are in real error or sin?

_____

_____

_____

Repentance

> Repent, then, and turn back, so that your sins may be wiped away, that times of refreshing may come from the presence of the Lord... (Acts 3:19-20)

What is the thing you must do, to be cleansed and refreshed?

_____

Where does this cleansing and refreshing come from? What is restored to you?

_____

What Repentance Looks Like

> And behold, there was a man called by the name of Zaccheus; and he was a chief tax-gatherer, and he was rich. And he was trying to see who Jesus was, and he was unable because of the crowd, for he was small in stature. And he ran on

ahead and climbed up into a sycamore tree in order to see Him, for He was about to pass through that way. And when Jesus came to the place, He looked up and said to him, "Zaccheus, hurry and come down, for today I must stay at your house." And he hurried and came down, and received Him gladly.

And when they saw it, they all began to grumble, saying, "He has gone to be the guest of a man who is a sinner." But Zaccheus stopped and said to the Lord, "Behold, Lord, half of my possessions I will give to the poor, and if I have defrauded anyone of anything, I will give back four times as much." And Jesus said to him, "Today salvation has come to this house, because he, too, is a son of Abraham." (Luke 19:2-10)

What did Zaccheus do when he repented?

_____

_____

Why does repaying or making restitution show repentance? What does it show about the heart?

_____

_____

Activation

Use the rest of this devotional time to consider: Is there anyone that you have wronged that you need to make it right with? Ask the Lord to reveal:

- ➤ If you need to make something right with your parents (Commandment 5)
- ➤ Anyone you have hurt sexually (Commandment 7)
- ➤ Anyone to whom you owe money or something else to; anything you have stolen that you can return or repay, anyone you have cheated (Commandment 8)
- ➤ Anyone you have lied to, or lied about (Commandment 9)
- ➤ Anyone you have hurt in any other way including hatred, lust, or defrauding (Commandments 5-10)
- ➤ Any other way you need to make something right with God (Commandments 1-4)

Make a decision that you will "make it right" to the best of your ability with those you have wronged in the past.

Then make a decision that you will continue to do so going forward—quickly, and with the Holy Spirit's prompting.

- ➤ You will walk in forgiveness, both receiving and extending.
- ➤ You will walk in love.
- ➤ You will walk in honor.
- ➤ You will walk in purity.
- ➤ You will walk in integrity.

Psalm 101

1 I will sing of your love and justice, LORD. I will praise you with songs.
2 I will be careful to live a blameless life— when will you come to help me?
I will lead a life of integrity in my own home.
3 I will refuse to look at anything vile and vulgar.
I hate all who deal crookedly; I will have nothing to do with them.
4 I will reject perverse ideas and stay away from every evil.
5 I will not tolerate people who slander their neighbors.
I will not endure conceit and pride.
6 I will search for faithful people to be my companions.
Only those who are above reproach will be allowed to serve me.
7 I will not allow deceivers to serve in my house, and liars will not stay in my presence.
8 My daily task will be to ferret out the wicked and free the city of the LORD from their grip.

PART III:
WALKING WITH GOD

LIVING IN CHRIST
Becoming Like Christ

> I count all things to be loss in view of the surpassing value of knowing Christ Jesus my Lord, for whom I have suffered the loss of all things. I count them but rubbish so that I may gain Christ, and may be found in Him, not having a righteousness of my own derived from the Law, but that which is through faith in Christ, the righteousness which comes from God on the basis of faith. (Philippians 3:8-9)

What is the point of turning away from all the things of the world? What do you get in return?

_____

_____

Does God love and accept you because you are "good enough"? Where does your goodness come from?

_____

_____

> For you died, and your life is now hidden with Christ in God. When Christ, who is our life, is revealed, then you also will be revealed with Him in glory. (Colossians 3:4)

How have you "died?"

_____

If your life is hidden, whose life is God looking at instead?

_____

If God sees you the same way he sees Jesus, then how does he see you? What was Jesus like?

_____

_____

Once you were alienated from God and were enemies in your minds because of your evil behavior. But now he has reconciled you by Christ's physical body through death to present you holy in his sight, without blemish and free from accusation— if you continue in your faith, established and firm, and do not move from the hope held out in the gospel. (Colossians 1:21-23)

Do you have to submit to alienating or tormenting thoughts anymore?

_____

What is the result if you stand firm and keep believing in the Gospel?

_____

_____

For I am convinced that neither death, nor life, nor angels, nor principalities, nor things present, nor things to come, nor powers, nor height, nor depth, nor any other created thing, will be able to separate us from the love of God, which is in Christ Jesus our Lord. (Romans 8:38-39)

When you're dealing with something hard—depression, failure, sin that's hard to beat—does it mean God withdrew from you?

_____

Can you do anything to stop God's love over your life? Name any you have believed have hindered it, and then cross them out with your pencil.

_____

_____

_____

But the one who joins himself to the Lord is one spirit with Him.
(1 Corinthians 6:17)

Whose nature do you now share?

_____

What do you have to do, to keep the Lord's righteousness as your own?

_____

Your New Identity

But as many as received Him, to them He gave the right to become sons of God, even to those who believe in His name. (John 1:12)

If you have been born again, what are you now?

_____

Who used to be your father? Who is your Father now?

_____

Knowing this, that our old self was crucified with Him, in order that our body of sin might be done away with, so that we would no longer be slaves to sin. (Romans 6:6)

Do you have to struggle with addictions or bad habits? Why not?

_____

_____

Therefore if anyone is in Christ, he is a new creature; the old things passed away; behold, new things have come! (2 Corinthians 5:17)

Whose nature is now living inside of you?

_____

If you have the nature of Christ inside of you, what does that mean about any evil or challenges in your past?

_____

_____

Put on the new man, which after God is created in righteousness and true holiness. (Ephesians 4:24)

Does the Bible tell you to just try harder, when you fail?

_____

What does this Scripture tell you to do, instead?

_____

> For he has rescued us from the dominion of darkness and brought us into the kingdom of the Son he loves, in whom we have redemption, the forgiveness of sins. (Colossians 1:13-14)

What is the nature of the new Kingdom you are part of now?

_____

_____

Who no longer has a right to touch you? Why not?

_____

_____

> God raised us up with Christ and seated us with Him in the heavenly places in Christ Jesus, in order that in the coming ages He might show the incomparable riches of his grace, expressed in his kindness to us in Christ Jesus. (Ephesians 2:6-8)

Where are you seated? Is this where you will be in the future, or where you are now?

_____

_____

Imagine this now for just a moment. Close your eyes. What is it like, to be seated with Him?

_____

_____

_____

> You are a chosen race, a royal priesthood, a holy nation, a people for God's own possession, so that you may proclaim the awesomeness of Him who has called you out of darkness into His marvelous light. (1 Peter 2:9)

Are you special? How special are you?

_____

_____

You have come out of darkness into what? Close your eyes and imagine what it is like to be there right now.

_____

_____

_____

Your Authority in Christ

In all these things, we are more than conquerors through Him who loved us. (Romans 8:37)

When you face trials, who will win?

_____

What kind of attitude is God encouraging you to have, if you are "more than a conqueror"?

_____

I can do all things through Christ who gives me strength. (Philippians 4:13)

Is there anything you cannot do, if you abide in Christ?

_____

But as many as received him, to them he gave power to become sons of God, even to them that believe on his name: Which were born, not of blood, nor of the will of the flesh, nor of the will of man, but of God. (John 1:12-13)

Jesus was the Son of God, but what does this say He gives you the power to be also?

_____

What comes with being a son of God?

_____

_____

> And these signs shall follow them that believe; In my name shall they cast out devils; they shall speak with new tongues; They shall take up serpents; and if they drink any deadly thing, it shall not hurt them; they shall lay hands on the sick, and they shall recover. (Mark 16:16-18)

What if you face demons? Should you be afraid? Who has the power in the battle?

_____

_____

What about death, sickness, or torment? Who has the power over those?

_____

What has God called you to do, with the power He gives you?

_____

_____

> Let us therefore approach God's throne of grace with confidence, so that we may receive mercy and find grace to help us in our time of need.
> (Hebrews 4:16)

How should you feel, when you ask things from God?

_____

Does God care about what you, personally, need?

_____

What kind of nature must God have, to feel this way?

_____

> Whatever you ask in My name, that will I do, so that the Father may be glorified in the Son. If you ask Me anything in My name, I will do it.   (John 14:13-14)

What will God give you if you ask?

_____

_____

Do you see any special qualifications here?

_____

_____

> This is the confidence we have in approaching God: that if we ask anything according to his will, he hears us. (1 John 5:14)

How does God want you to approach Him?

_____

Does God want you to ask Him for what you need?

_____

Have you ever felt like God didn't hear your prayers? Because you are in Christ, what are you promised?

_____

_____

> Jesus answered and said to them, "Truly I say to you, if you have faith and do not doubt, you will not only do what was done to the fig tree, but even if you say to this mountain, 'Be taken up and cast into the sea,' it will happen. And all things you ask in prayer, believing, you will receive." (Matthew 21:20-22)

Do you have authority to obtain what you need?

_____

How many things can you obtain?

_____

Will you receive what you asked for?

_____

Where Power Comes From

If you remain in me and my words remain in you, ask whatever you wish, and it will be done for you. (John 15:7)

What is the condition to receiving answers to prayer, and power in God?

_____

_____

What can you ask for, if you are in Him?

_____

_____

My prayer is not for them alone. I pray also for those who will believe in me through their message, that all of them may be one, Father, just as you are in me and I am in you. May they also be in us so that the world may believe that you have sent me. I have given them the glory that you gave me, that they may be one as we are one—I in them and you in me—so that they may be brought to complete unity. (John 17:20-23)

Are you alone anymore? Who is in you? Who are you "in"?

_____

In terms of relationship, what is the end result of following God?

_____

_____

I am the true vine, and my Father is the gardener. He cuts off every branch in me that bears no fruit, while every branch that does bear fruit he prunes so that it will be even more fruitful. You are already clean because of the word I have spoken to you. Remain in me, as I also remain in you. No branch can bear fruit by itself; it must remain in the vine. Neither can you bear fruit unless you remain in me. (John 15:1-4)

How connected does Jesus want to be?

_____

_____

Do you have to try hard to bear fruit? What enables you to bear good fruit?

_____

_____

Based on this, do you think you should be focusing more on doing good works, or on knowing Jesus better?

_____

How can trying to do good works become a trap?

_____

_____

_____

> I am the vine; you are the branches. If you remain in me and I in you, you will bear much fruit; apart from me you can do nothing. If you do not remain in me, you are like a branch that is thrown away and withers; such branches are picked up, thrown into the fire and burned. If you remain in me and my words remain in you, ask whatever you wish, and it will be done for you. This is to my Father's glory, that you bear much fruit, showing yourselves to be my disciples. (John 15:5-8)

Is there anything good you can do apart from Jesus?

_____

How often does Jesus want to be with you?

_____

How do you (honestly) feel when you think about the goal of having Jesus with you, all day, all the time, in everything you do?

_____

_____

Do you need to make any changes in your heart, to allow someone to be that close to you? Pray and ask the Lord to reveal them, if so.

_____

_____

_____

HEALING

God's Will for Healing

> I am the Lord who heals you. (Exodus 15:26)

Many people believe that God gives them illness to teach them things, or that He "allows" them to be sick. On the contrary, what does this verse say about God's nature?

_____

_____

Could God have said this honestly, if He desires to place sickness on people, for any reason?

_____

_____

> The thief comes to steal, to kill, and to destroy. I came so that they might have life and have it more abundantly. (John 10:10).

What does sickness and disease do to many people?

_____

_____

Do you think that an "abundant" life includes sickness and disease?

_____

_____

How does sickness relate to "stealing, killing, and destroying"?

_____

_____

If sickness kills and destroys your body, is it the work of God or the work of Satan?

_____

Jesus came to destroy the works of the devil. (1 John 3:8)

If sickness is the work of the devil, what did Jesus come in order to do to it?

_____

Healing in the Atonement

Surely He took up our pain and bore our suffering, yet we considered Him punished by God, stricken by him and afflicted. But He was pierced for our transgressions, He was crushed for our iniquities. The punishment that brought us peace was upon Him, and by His wounds we are healed. (Isaiah 53:4-5)

Jesus suffered for your sins, but what other benefit came right alongside spiritual healing?

_____

What did Jesus "take up" on the Cross?

_____

What did Jesus' pain purchase for you?

_____

Praise the Lord, O my soul, and forget not all his benefits; who forgives all your sins and heals all your diseases. (Psalm 103:2-3).

Salvation means that God forgives your sins, but what else does it mean?

_____

What sicknesses can God not heal?

_____

Does God Want Only Some to be Healed?

When evening came, they brought to Him many who were demon-possessed; and He cast out the spirits with a word, and healed **all** who were ill. This was to fulfill what was spoken through Isaiah the prophet: 'He Himself took our infirmities and carried away our diseases.' (Matthew 8:16-17)

114

How many did Jesus heal, when He came?

_____

Did He ask any questions? Were there any prerequisites to receiving healing?

_____

Did He heal only physical illnesses?

_____

Why did Jesus heal them all?

_____

_____

A large crowd followed Him, and He healed **all** who were ill. (Matthew 12:15)

How many from the crowd did Jesus heal?

_____

Did He exclude any, for any reason?

_____

Were any of these people noted as special, for any reason? What kind of people were these?

_____

At sunset, the people brought to Jesus **all** who had various kinds of illnesses, and laying His hands on **each one**, He healed them. (Luke 4:40).

How many did Jesus heal, that were brought to Him?

_____

Did He distinguish between any kind of people or situations?

_____

Were any conditions too hard? Did anyone deserve their illness?

_____

Did Jesus say anything or teach anything before giving them what they needed?

_____

Did anyone have to do anything first, before they could be healed? Or tell Him anything?

_____

How did He heal them?

_____

> Jesus went throughout Galilee, teaching in their synagogues, proclaiming the good news of the kingdom, and healing **every** disease and sickness among the people. News about him spread all over Syria, and people brought to him **all who were ill** with various diseases, those suffering severe pain, the demon-possessed, those having seizures, and the paralyzed; and he healed them. (Matthew 4:23-24)

How many did Jesus heal in the synagogue (or church)?

_____

Was there any kind of condition that He did not heal?

_____

Did it need to be clear what He was healing, before it could be healed?

_____

> And great crowds came to Him, bringing with them the lame, the blind, the crippled, the mute, and many others, and they put them at His feet, and He healed them, so that the crowd wondered, when they saw the mute speaking, the crippled healthy, the lame walking, and the blind seeing. And they glorified the God of Israel. (Matthew 15:30-31)

Were there any cases Jesus didn't heal?

_____

Did He make anyone wait?

_____

What about those with very difficult cases? Strange, incurable, contagious, congenital conditions...?

> In one of the villages, Jesus met a man with an advanced case of leprosy. When the man saw Jesus, he bowed with his face to the ground, begging to be healed. "Lord," he said, "if you are willing, you can heal me and make me clean." Jesus reached out and touched him. "I am willing," he said. "Be healed!" And instantly the leprosy disappeared. (Luke 5:12-13)

What do you imagine a man's condition with "advanced leprosy" would be like?

This man doubted that was God's will to heal him. What did Jesus specifically declare God's will is, for healing?

Did He hesitate?

Did Jesus just declare that He was (theoretically) willing, or did He do more?

Who Can Heal the Sick?

> Heal the sick, raise the dead, cure those with leprosy, and cast out demons. Freely you have received, so freely give. (Matthew 10:8)

Did Jesus command His followers to keep healing?

Whom were they supposed to go and pray for?

Would He have told His followers to do something they couldn't do?

_____

> And God has placed **in the church** first of all apostles, second prophets, third teachers, then miracles, then gifts of **healing**, of helping, of guidance, and of different kinds of tongues. (1 Corinthians 12:28)

Where did God want His power of healing to rest/live, after Jesus left?

_____

Does God make healing sound like a fantastical gift, out of proportion with the other gifts in the church?

_____

_____

> "Teacher," said John, "we saw someone driving out demons in your name and we told him to stop, because he was not one of us." "Do not stop him," Jesus said. "For no one who does a miracle in my name can in the next moment say anything bad about me, for whoever is not against us is for us." (Mark 9:38-40)

Did only those specifically sent out by Jesus Himself receive the power to heal others?

_____

> Is **anyone** among you sick? Then he must call for the **elders** of the church and they are to pray over him, anointing him with oil in the name of the Lord. And the prayer offered in faith will make the sick person well; the Lord will raise them up. If they have sinned, they will be forgiven. (James 5:14-15)

Who should receive prayer for healing?

_____

Was the power to heal given only to the original disciples right around Jesus?

_____

_____

What is the only behavior attached to receiving healing?

_____

Who is told to have faith? The sick person, or the person who prays?

_____

What about if the sickness is attached to a sinful lifestyle?

_____

How to Minister Healing

So He bent over her and rebuked the fever, and it left her. (Luke 4:39)

How did Jesus pray for healing?

_____

Was it long and complex?

_____

So they brought him. When the spirit saw Jesus, it immediately threw the boy into a convulsion. He fell to the ground and rolled around, foaming at the mouth... When Jesus saw that a crowd was running to the scene, he rebuked the impure spirit. "You deaf and mute spirit," he said, "I command you, come out of him and never enter him again!" (Mark 9:20, 25)

Did Jesus "ask" for healing?

_____

What did He do?

_____

What power was behind the boy's illness?

_____

Did Jesus feel intimidated by this?

_____

He took along the child's father and mother and His own companions, and entered the room where the child was. Taking the child by the hand, He said to her, "Talitha kum!" (which translated means, "Little girl, I say to you, get up!"). Immediately the girl got up and began to walk...(Mark 5:40-42)

Did Jesus "ask" for healing? What did He do instead?

_____

Was He intimidated about how far gone the little girl was?

_____

If you act like Jesus, how will you treat sickness?

_____

HEARING GOD
The God Who Speaks

You know that when you were pagans, somehow or other you were influenced and led astray to mute idols. (1 Corinthians 12:2)

If idols are "mute," then what is the real God?

_____

For I did not speak on my own, but the Father who sent Me commanded Me to say all that I have spoken. (John 12:49)

Who is the originator of all Jesus said?

_____

"But when he, the Spirit of truth, comes, he will guide you into all the truth. He will not speak on his own; he will speak only what he hears, and he will tell you what is yet to come." (John 16:13)

What is God's special gift to His children, so they can hear what He says?

_____

What is the Holy Spirit speaking?

_____

"He who has ears to hear, let him hear!" (Mt. 11:15, 13:9, 13:43; Mk. 4:9, Mk. 4:23, Lk. 8:8, Lk. 14:35)

Is God talking about physical hearing? What is He talking about?

_____

_____

Jesus says this same thing in at least seven different verses. Why do you think this hearing is so important?

_____

If two people receive the same teaching, what is the difference between someone who "hears" it and someone who doesn't?

_____

_____

My sheep hear my voice, and I know them, and they follow me.   (John 10:27)

What does God promise His followers?

_____

Do you have to worry that you don't hear God?

_____

What kinds of things might a shepherd "say" or communicate to his sheep?

_____

_____

Do sheep have to understand human language in order to know what their shepherd is telling them? Why not?

_____

_____

Then the Lord called Samuel. Samuel answered, "Here I am." And he ran to Eli and said, "Here I am; you called me." But Eli said, "I did not call; go back and lie down." So he went and lay down. Again the Lord called, "Samuel!" And Samuel got up and went to Eli and said, "Here I am; you called me." "My son," Eli said, "I did not call; go back and lie down." Now Samuel did not yet know the Lord: The word of the Lord had not yet been revealed to him. A third time the Lord called, "Samuel!" And Samuel got up and went to Eli and said, "Here I am; you called me."

Then Eli realized that the Lord was calling the **boy**. So Eli told Samuel, "Go and lie down, and if he calls you, say, 'Speak, Lord, for your servant is listening.' " So Samuel went and lay down in his place. The Lord came and stood there, calling as at the other times, "Samuel! Samuel!" Then Samuel said, "Speak, for your servant is listening." (1 Samuel 3:4-10)

Did God reach out to Samuel first, or did Samuel reach out to God first?

_____

Did God choose someone particularly old and wise to speak to? Or someone inexperienced but willing?

_____

Did God give up on speaking to Samuel just because he didn't understand Him the first time?

_____

How did Samuel respond when he finally realized it was God? What did God want to hear, before He said more?

_____

_____

Did Samuel need help to discern the voice of the Lord? Is it ok if you do?

_____

As Moses went into the tent, the pillar of cloud would come down and stay at the entrance while the Lord spoke with Moses... The Lord would speak to Moses face to face, as one speaks to a friend... (Exodus 33:9-11)

What is the ultimate goal of communing with Jesus, or spending time with Him?

_____

How do friends normally speak to one another? How often do they usually speak?

_____

_____

How is reading your Bible similar to speaking to God "face to face, as one speaks to a friend?"

_____

_____

What others ways can you and God communicate as friends?

_____

_____

Words of Knowledge

As For we know in part and we prophesy in part, but when the perfect comes, the partial will pass away...Now we see in a mirror dimly, but then face to face; now I know in part, but then I will know fully, just as I also have been fully known." (1 Corinthians 13:9-12)

In the end, in heaven, we will finally see God face to face. What will happen to prophecy—the need to hear God and speak for Him—at that point?

_____

What has to keep going on until then?

_____

"For to one is given the word of wisdom through the Spirit, and to another the word of knowledge according to the same Spirit." (1 Corinthians 12:8)

What two components of prophecy are mentioned here?

_____

Whose knowledge and wisdom are being revealed in "words of knowledge" and "words of wisdom"?

_____

What does God giving us "words" mean about His nature...today?

_____

_____

Then the man and his wife heard the **sound** of the LORD God walking in the garden in the cool of the day, and the man and his wife hid themselves from the presence of the LORD God among the trees of the garden. Then the LORD God **called** to the man, and said to him, "Where are you?" Adam **answered**, "I **heard** you in the garden, and I was afraid because I was naked; so I hid." And the LORD said, "Who told you that you were naked? Have you eaten from the tree that I commanded you not to eat from?" (Genesis 3:8-11)

God had the first "word of knowledge" in the Bible. What was it?

_____

What was the word of knowledge meant to do? What is God's attitude towards secret behavior?

_____

_____

What question is God's prophetic voice always calling out, even if we're hiding? What is the purpose of corrective prophecy?

_____

_____

Throughout Scripture, God's *voice* indicates His presence. Could Adam and Eve hear it, even after they sinned? What does this mean for you? For the lost?

_____

_____

When Jesus saw Nathanael approaching, He said of him, 'Here truly is an Israelite in whom there is no deceit.' 'How do you know me?' Nathanael asked. Jesus answered, 'I saw you while you were still under the fig tree before Philip called you.' Then Nathanael declared, 'Rabbi, you are the Son of God; you are the king of Israel.' (John 1:47-49)

Had Nathanael met Jesus before?

_____

How did Jesus "see" Nathanael earlier?

_____

What revelation did Nathanael receive in return, after Jesus gave His?

_____

What was Jesus' prophetic declaration about Nathanael's identity? Was it positive or negative in tone?

_____

_____

> He [Jesus] told her [the woman at the well], "Go, call your husband and come back." "I have no husband," she replied. Jesus said to her, 'You are right when you say you have no husband. The fact is, you have had five husbands, and the man you now have is not your husband. What you have just said is quite true.' 'Sir,' the woman said, 'I can see that you are a prophet.'" (John 4:16-19)

Jesus had a word of knowledge about the woman's five husbands. What did this word release her to see?

_____

Do you think the woman felt judged by Jesus' revelation? What was Jesus' purpose in prophesying to her?

_____

_____

> Now a man named Ananias, together with his wife Sapphira, also sold a piece of property. With his wife's full knowledge he kept back part of the money for himself, but brought the rest and put it at the apostles' feet. Then Peter said, "Ananias, how is it that Satan has so filled your heart that you have lied to the Holy Spirit and have kept for yourself some of the money you received for the land? Didn't it belong to you before it was sold? And after it was sold, wasn't the money at your disposal? What made you think of doing such a thing? You have not lied just to human beings but to God. (Acts 5:1-5)

Who received this word of knowledge? Was Jesus the only one whom the Holy Spirit could reveal things to?

_____

Did anyone know the truth of what Ananias and Sapphira did?

_____

They were presenting a certain amount of charity as an act of the Holy Spirit before the Christian community. Whom were they lying to? Who revealed their lie?

_____

_____

How can a prophetic act protect a church community?

_____

_____

> Following after Paul and us, she kept crying out, saying, 'These men are bond-servants of the Most High God, who are proclaiming to you the way of salvation.' She continued doing this for many days. But Paul was greatly annoyed, and turned and said to the spirit, 'I command you in the name of Jesus Christ to come out of her!' And it came out at that very moment. (Acts 16:17-18)

At the outset, it seemed like the woman following Paul was just an eager and vocal follower of God. However, Paul discerned by the Holy Spirit that she had what?

_____

How can a prophetic word restore order to the church?

_____

_____

> Paul and his companions traveled throughout the region of Phrygia and Galatia, having been kept by the Holy Spirit from preaching the word in the province of Asia. When they came to the border of Mysia, they tried to enter Bithynia, but the Spirit of Jesus would not allow them to. So they passed by Mysia and went down to Troas. During the night Paul had a vision of a man of Macedonia standing and begging him, "Come over to Macedonia and help us." After Paul had seen the vision, we got ready at once to leave for Macedonia, concluding that God had called us to preach the gospel to them. (Acts 16:6-10)

What word of knowledge did the Holy Spirit reveal to Paul as he planned his mission trips?

_____

_____

Paul went to Macedonia where he reached the Philippians and wrote that book of Scripture. How can prophecy aid the spread of the gospel?

_____

_____

The Gift of Prophecy

> The one who prophesies speaks to people for their strengthening, encouraging and comfort. (1 Corinthians 14:3)

What is prophesying?

_____

_____

Is it predicting the End Times or cataclysmic doom?

_____

Is it something that only super special people have knowledge about?

_____

> Anyone who speaks in a tongue edifies themselves, but the one who prophesies edifies the church. I would like **every one** of you to speak in tongues, **but I would rather have you prophesy**. The one who prophesies is greater than the one who speaks in tongues, unless someone interprets, so that the church may be edified. (1 Corinthians 14:4-5)

Is prophecy for today?

_____

Is it for everyone? Is it for you?

_____

Why is it so important? What is its purpose?

_____

Try to excel in those that build up the church. (1 Corinthians 14:12)

How does God want His people to feel?

_____

What is God expecting His followers throughout history, to face?

_____

Can we get better at prophecy?

_____

If the whole church comes together and everyone speaks in tongues, and inquirers or unbelievers come in, will they not say that you are out of your mind? But if an unbeliever or an inquirer comes in while everyone is prophesying, they are convicted of sin and are brought under judgment by all, as the secrets of their hearts are laid bare. So they will fall down and worship God, exclaiming, "God is really among you! (1 Corinthians 14:23-25)

What does Paul imagine "the whole church" and "everyone" doing while at church?

_____

What spiritual gift can speak well to unbelievers?

_____

What is the effect of prophecy properly done in the church?

_____

_____

Therefore, my brothers and sisters, be eager to prophesy, and do not forbid speaking in tongues. But everything should be done in a fitting and orderly way. (1 Corinthians14:39-40)

Paul has some specific instructions regarding how to keep spiritual gifts "fitting and orderly," but his main point is that we all can do what?

_____

The Spirit searches all things, even the deep things of God. For who knows a person's thoughts except their own spirit within them? In the same way no one knows the thoughts of God except the Spirit of God. (1 Corinthians 2:10-11)

129

The purpose of prophecy is to disclose what?

_____

How does prophecy act as a connector of people and God?

_____

> To one there is given through the Spirit a message of wisdom, to another a message of knowledge by means of the same Spirit, to another faith by the same Spirit, to another gifts of healing by that one Spirit, to another miraculous powers, to another prophecy, to another distinguishing between spirits, to another speaking in different kinds of tongues, and to still another the interpretation of tongues." (1 Corinthians 12:8-10)

> Now you are the Body of Christ, and **each one of you** is a part of it. And God has placed in the church first of all apostles, second prophets, third teachers, then miracles, then gifts of healing, of helping, of guidance, and of different kinds of tongues." (1 Corinthians 12:27-28)

Is prophecy obsolete? Did it die out with Christ and the apostles?

_____

Has teaching, helping, guidance died out?

_____

Is prophecy supposed to be part of church life? What kinds of things did God envision going on in a believing community?

_____

_____

The Corinthians were a believing group in Greece. Who are these passages addressed to? A special class of people?

_____

Does Paul indicate that "prophets" here are a select group of people, distinct from believers in the Body?

_____

Now eagerly desire the greater gifts. (1 Corinthians 12:31)

Follow the way of love and pursue gifts of the Spirit, especially prophecy... For you can all prophesy in turn so that everyone may be instructed and encouraged. (1 Corinthians 14:1)

Based on this, why is prophecy considered one of the "greater gifts"?

_____

_____

How does prophecy encourage "following the way of love?"

_____

_____

Did God predestine you to have just one gift you didn't choose, or can you achieve other spiritual gifts in your lifetime?

_____

How much should we desire and pursue the gifts God has for us?

_____

AVOIDING WORLDLY TRAPS
Jesus Versus the World

> Greater is He that is in me, than he that is in the world. (1 John 4:4)

What two systems on earth are there? Who are the leaders of those systems?

_____

_____

Are these systems compatible or opposed?

_____

Which one is meant to overcome?

_____

> He who loves his life will lose it; and he who hates his life in this world shall keep it to life eternal. (John 12:25)

What will happen if you love your own life?

_____

How should you handle your own pursuits and goals?

_____

> This I command you, that you love one another. If the world hates you, you know that it has hated Me before it hated you. If you were of the world, the world would love its own; but because you are not of the world, but I chose you out of the world, therefore the world hates you. Remember the word that I said to you, 'A slave is not greater than his master.' If they persecuted Me, they will also persecute you; if they kept My word, they will keep yours also. But all these things they will do to you for My name's sake, because they do not know the One who sent Me. (John 15:17-21)

If people in the world love you, is that a good sign?

_____

How will people in the world treat true disciples of Jesus? Will you always win them over?

_____

_____

What makes those who hate you, do so? Is it you?

_____

If no-one ever rejects you because of your beliefs, what might this mean?

_____

_____

Blessed are you when men cast insults at you, and persecute you, and say all kinds of evil against you falsely, on account of Me. Rejoice, and be glad, for your reward in heaven is great, for so they persecuted the prophets who were before you. (Matthew 5:11-12)

How should you feel when you are rejected on behalf of Jesus?

_____

What do you gain when you lose in this life, because of Jesus?

_____

_____

"For I came to set a man against his father, and a daughter against her mother, and a daughter-in-law against her mother-in-law; and a man's enemies will be the members of his household. He who loves father or mother more than Me is not worthy of Me; and he who loves son or daughter more than Me is not worthy of Me. (Matthew 10:35-37)

Who may turn against you because of your decision to follow Jesus?

_____

_____

_____

You may be tempted or coerced to put family relationships above your commitment to Jesus. What does Jesus say about those who do this?

_____

_____

> Brother will deliver up brother to death, and a father his child; and children will rise up against parents, and cause them to be put to death. And you will be hated by all on account of My name, but it is the one who has endured to the end who will be saved. (Matthew 10:21-22)

What is the one thing God asks you to do in the face of hatred?

_____

> And he who does not take his cross and follow after Me is not worthy of Me. He who has found his life shall lose it, and he who has lost his life for My sake shall find it. (Matthew 10:38-39)

What does God promise those who are persecuted?

_____

The World's Situation

> The wrath of God is being revealed from heaven against all the godlessness and wickedness of people, who suppress the truth by their wickedness, since what may be known about God is plain to them, because God has made it plain to them. For since the creation of the world God's invisible qualities—his eternal power and divine nature—have been clearly seen, being understood from what has been made, so that people are without excuse. For although they knew God, they neither glorified him as God nor gave thanks to him, but their thinking became futile and their foolish hearts were darkened. Although they claimed to be wise, they became fools and exchanged the glory of the immortal God for images made to look like a mortal human being and birds and animals and reptiles.
>
> Therefore God gave them over in the sinful desires of their hearts to sexual impurity for the degrading of their bodies with one another. They exchanged the truth about God for a lie, and worshiped and served created things rather than the Creator—who is forever praised. Amen. Because of this, God gave them over to shameful lusts. Even their women exchanged natural sexual relations for unnatural ones. In the same way the men also abandoned natural relations with

women and were inflamed with lust for one another. Men committed shameful acts with other men, and received in themselves the due penalty for their error.

Furthermore, just as they did not think it worthwhile to retain the knowledge of God, so God gave them over to a depraved mind, so that they do what ought not to be done. They have become filled with every kind of wickedness, evil, greed and depravity. They are full of envy, murder, strife, deceit and malice. They are gossips, slanderers, God-haters, insolent, arrogant and boastful; they invent ways of doing evil; they disobey their parents; they have no understanding, no fidelity, no love, no mercy. Although they know God's righteous decree that those who do such things deserve death, they not only continue to do these very things but also approve of those who practice them.   (Romans 1:18-32)

How is it clear there is a God, even to those who do not believe?

_____

_____

How do most people respond to the facts they have about God?

_____

_____

What kind of religion results when people refuse to respond to that truth?

_____

_____

What kinds of things do people do to satisfy their desires, once they have gotten far enough away from God?

_____

_____

_____

What happens when someone turns far enough away from God?

_____

_____

How does an entire society become hateful of God?

_____

_____

Based on this passage, how do wrong ideas about God and evil practices go together?

_____

_____

Mark this: There will be terrible times in the last days. People will be lovers of themselves, lovers of money, boastful, proud, abusive, disobedient to their parents, ungrateful, unholy, without love, unforgiving, slanderous, without self-control, brutal, not lovers of the good, treacherous, rash, conceited, lovers of pleasure rather than lovers of God— having a form of godliness but denying its power. Have nothing to do with such people. (2 Timothy 3:1-5)

Do you see these things around you today?

_____

How are these things promoted?

_____

_____

Pressure to conform to the world's attitudes may come in the form of an actual person, or in what other ways?

_____

_____

How does this verse instruct you to overcome worldly pressure or influence?

_____

_____

Just became something seems good or godly, does that mean it truly is good? How do you know?

_____

_____

If you are being corrupted by worldly company, what does God ask you to do?

_____

> For among them are those who worm their way into homes and captivate weak women weighed down with sins and led astray by various passions, who are swayed by all kinds of evil desires, always learning but never able to come to a knowledge of the truth. (2 Timothy 3:6-7)

Does reading or learning more always lead to truth? Why not?

_____

_____

Can you think of anyone who knows more than you, or always learning more, but is clearly deceived?

_____

_____

What does this verse tell you about relying on your own intelligence or study habits for guidance?

_____

_____

In this passage, what is a temptation for male leaders in society? What is a weakness for many women?

_____

_____

False Teaching

From the least to the greatest, all are greedy for gain; prophets and priests alike, all practice deceit. They dress the wound of my people as though it were not serious. 'Peace, peace,' they say, when there is no peace. Are they ashamed of their detestable conduct? No, they have no shame at all; they do not even know how to blush. So they will fall among the fallen; they will be brought down when I punish them. (Jeremiah 6:13)

False teachers and prophets always preach self-gratification when the real problem is what?

_____

_____

What is the end result of following the lies of the false prophets of your generation?

_____

_____

The time will come when people will not put up with sound doctrine. Instead, to suit their own desires, they will gather around them a great number of teachers to say what their itching ears want to hear. They will turn their ears away from the truth and turn aside to myths. (2 Timothy 4:3-4)

How can you tell you are listening to a myth made up to suit "itching ears"?

_____

_____

What sources are the "teachers" in our culture, that tell us what to believe?

_____

_____

_____

Can these sources be trusted?

_____

See to it that no one takes you captive through hollow and deceptive philosophy, which depends on human tradition and the elemental spiritual forces of this world rather than on Christ. (Colossians 2:8)

What can you be taken captive by?

_____

_____

Even if something sounds intelligent, if it is not based on God, what is it based on?

_____

_____

Are there any philosophies or theories that people commonly believe around you, that God is leading you in a different direction?

_____

_____

How does the Bible describe these philosophies which are not based on Christ?

_____

_____

So also we, while we were children, were held in bondage under the basic principles of the world...Formerly, when you did not know God, you were slaves to those who by nature are not gods. But now that you know God--or rather are known by God--how is it that you are turning back to those weak and miserable forces? Do you wish to be enslaved by them all over again? (Galatians 4:3, 8-9)

"Basic principles of the world" are not complex philosophies but popular ideas and ways of life. What are some of the "basic principles" of the world around you?

_____

_____

_____

_____

Where do these ideas lead?

_____

When you follow Christ, He asks you to reject these principles, but what is the temptation?

_____

_____

> You gladly put up with fools since you are so wise! In fact, you even put up with anyone who enslaves you or exploits you or takes advantage of you or puts on airs or slaps you in the face. (2 Corinthians 11:9-20)

According to this verse, those who teach false doctrines do not only seduce you, what else will they do to keep you from the truth?

_____

_____

> Timothy, guard what has been entrusted to your care. Turn away from godless chatter and the opposing ideas of what is falsely called knowledge, which some have professed and thus gone astray from the faith." (1 Timothy 6:20-21).

Sometimes people think they have found a secret key of "knowledge" about something. Where does this lead?

_____

"Godless chatter" is meaningless talk about worldly things. It may seem harmless, but where does it lead?

_____

What kinds of things might you personally have to do, to avoid sources of "godless chatter"?

_____

_____

> We destroy arguments and every lofty opinion raised against the knowledge of God, and take every thought captive to obey Christ. (2 Corinthians 10:5)

Do you run away from false ideas? What is our job, as Christians, when we run into them?

_____

_____

Does this sound like something you can do passively?

_____

_____

What practical things can you to do, to escape having worldly thoughts?

_____

_____

_____

_____

This verse indicates that your thoughts and ideas need to "obey" Christ, just like your behavior. Which do you think the bigger war is?

_____

Why?

_____

_____

What is the ultimate standard of Truth by which you can judge all arguments?

_____

Common Traps

> But I am afraid that as the serpent deceived Eve by his cunning, your thoughts will be led astray from a sincere and pure devotion to Christ. For if someone comes and proclaims another Jesus than the one we proclaimed, or if you receive a different spirit from the one you received, or if you accept a different gospel from the one you accepted, you put up with it readily enough. (2 Corinthians 11:3-4)

What are the three situations that Paul links to being the same kind of deception that befell Adam and Eve?

_____

_____

_____

If the only way to heaven is through Jesus' love for us, and His death on the Cross, what is the mark of a false gospel?

_____

_____

> Therefore do not let anyone judge you by what you eat or drink, or with regard to a religious festival, a New Moon celebration, or a Sabbath day. These are a shadow of the things that were to come; the reality, however, is found in Christ.

What kinds of things does Paul say not to get caught up in?

_____

_____

In what ways have you seen that these are popular fascinations today?

_____

_____

Why aren't we to get caught up in these things?

_____

_____

> Do not let anyone who delights in false humility and the worship of angels disqualify you. Such a person also goes into great detail about what they have seen; they are puffed up with idle notions by their unspiritual mind. They have lost connection with the Head, from whom the whole body, supported and held together by its ligaments and sinews, grows as God causes it to grow (Colossians 2:18-19)

What kinds of things does Paul say not to get caught up in here?

_____

_____

What is the problem with those who are continually transfixed by spiritual experiences and what God told them?

_____

_____

> If you have died with Christ to the spiritual forces of the world, why, as though you still belonged to the world, do you submit to its regulations: "Do not handle, do not taste, do not touch!"? These will all perish with use, because they are based on human commands and teachings. Such restrictions indeed have an appearance of wisdom, with their self-prescribed worship, their false humility, and their harsh treatment of the body; but they are of no value against the indulgence of the flesh. (Colossians 2:20-23)

Does eating a healthy diet make you a better person?

_____

Does avoiding certain foods, chemicals, or lifestyle practices make you more spiritual?

_____

Why doesn't punishing yourself, imposing rigid regulations on yourself, or subjecting your body to "harsh treatment" work?

_____

_____

_____

BEING A WITNESS
Reaching the Lost

There was a rich man who was clothed in purple and fine linen and who feasted sumptuously every day. And at his gate was laid a poor man named Lazarus, covered with sores, who desired to be fed with what fell from the rich man's table. Moreover, even the dogs came and licked his sores. The poor man died and was carried by the angels to Abraham's side.

The rich man also died and was buried, and in Hades, being in torment, he lifted up his eyes and saw Abraham far off and Lazarus at his side. And he called out, 'Father Abraham, have mercy on me, and send Lazarus to dip the end of his finger in water and cool my tongue, for I am in anguish in this flame.' But Abraham said, 'Child, remember that you in your lifetime received your good things, and Lazarus in like manner bad things; but now he is comforted here, and you are in anguish. And besides all this, between us and you a great chasm has been fixed, in order that those who would pass from here to you may not be able, and none may cross from there to us.' And the rich man said, 'Then I beg you, father, to send him to my father's house— for I have five brothers—so that he may warn them, lest they also come into this place of torment...' (Luke 16:19-28)

How does the Bible describe hell?

_____

_____

Can people get out of it once they are there?

_____

What is the one thing the man in hell begs for?

_____

_____

What is the only thing that can save his family?

_____

How can you be the hero in this story?

_____

_____

> In their case the god of this world has blinded the minds of the unbelievers, to keep them from seeing the light of the gospel of the glory of Christ, who is the image of God... For God, who said, "Let light shine out of darkness," made his light shine in our hearts. (2 Corinthians 4:4, 6)

What is the spiritual condition of the world, without the gospel?

_____

Who is responsible for consigning people to hell?

_____

What is God's response to that?

_____

_____

In light of eternity in heaven or hell, does anything else compare in significance?

_____

What do you think is the main thing on God's mind every day?

_____

Why Jesus Came

> So He told them this parable: "What man of you, having a hundred sheep, if he has lost one of them, does not leave the ninety-nine in the open country, and go after the one that is lost, until he finds it? And when he has found it, he lays it on his shoulders, rejoicing. And when he comes home, he calls together his friends and his neighbors, saying to them, 'Rejoice with me, for I have found my sheep that was lost.' Just so, I tell you, there will be more joy in heaven over one sinner who repents than over ninety-nine righteous persons who need no repentance." (Luke 15:3-7)

How does Jesus feel about rescuing people?

_____

_____

What is He willing to do, to rescue even one?

_____

_____

What happens when you rescue someone? Why?

_____

_____

How do you think Jesus feels about people who are out in the world alone?

_____

_____

What does God calling them "lost" imply about their belonging?

_____

_____

Jesus went throughout all the cities and villages, teaching in their synagogues and proclaiming the gospel of the kingdom and healing every disease and every affliction. When He saw the crowds, He had compassion for them, because they were harassed and helpless, like sheep without a shepherd. (Matthew 9:35-36).

How does a shepherd care for his sheep? Does he like them? What is his main job?

_____

_____

How did Jesus feel about people? Did He blame them? Judge them? Why not?

_____

_____

What was Jesus' attitude? Did He go to just some places? Did He turn any crowds away?

_____

_____

> I am the Good Shepherd. The good shepherd lays his life down for the sheep. (John 10:11)

If you are like Jesus, what will you do for people?

_____

> It is not the healthy who need a doctor, but the sick. (Mark 2:17).

Why does Jesus liken sinners to those who are sick?

_____

_____

> For the Son of Man has come to seek and to save that which was lost. (Luke 19:10)

What does it mean to "save the lost"? Who is lost, and how can they be saved?

_____

_____

What was Jesus' purpose in coming to earth?

_____

_____

What should your own life mission center around?

_____

_____

Our Commission

> While walking by the Sea of Galilee, He [Jesus] saw two brothers, Simon (who is called Peter) and Andrew his brother, casting a net into the sea, for they were fishermen. And He said to them, "Follow me, and I will make you fishers of men. (Matthew 4:18-19)

This was Jesus' very first command to His followers. What did He mean by calling them "fishers of men"? What was Jesus going to train them to do?

_____

_____

As followers of Jesus, what is one of the very first things He wants us to do?

_____

How do you currently do that?

_____

> And Jesus came and said to them, "All authority in heaven and on earth has been given to me. Go therefore and make disciples of all nations, baptizing them in the name of the Father and of the Son and of the Holy Spirit, teaching them to observe all that I have commanded you. And behold, I am with you always, to the end of the age. (Matt. 28:18-20)

This is Jesus' last command to His followers. Did Jesus ask them to be nice people and go to church?

_____

What did He send them out to do?

_____

How far were they supposed to go? How long were they supposed to preach?

_____

_____

How much authority was available to get their job done?

_____

_____

Many things must be done to disciple the nations, but what should every true Christian activity come back to?

_____

> But you will receive power when the Holy Spirit has come upon you, and you will be my witnesses in Jerusalem and in all Judea and Samaria, and to the ends of the earth." (Acts 1:8)

What is a witness? What does a witness promise to tell?

_____

_____

Was the power of the Holy Spirit given for just personal growth?

_____

_____

> And they sang a new song, saying, 'Worthy are you to take the scroll and to open its seals, for you were slain, and by your blood you ransomed people for God from every tribe and language and people and nation.' (Revelation 5:9)

Jesus died on the Cross to purchase which people?

_____

Has "every tribe and language and people and nation" been reached yet?

_____

What does this mean about our mission?

_____

_____

I charge you in the presence of God and of Christ Jesus, who is to judge the living and the dead, and by his appearing and his kingdom: preach the word; be ready in season and out of season; reprove, rebuke, and exhort, with complete patience and teaching...always be sober-minded, endure suffering, do the work of an evangelist, fulfill your ministry. (2 Timothy 4:1-5)

What kinds of things does God ask His ministers to do?

_____

_____

Since, then, we know what it is to fear the Lord, we try to persuade others...All this is from God, who reconciled us to himself through Christ and gave us the ministry of reconciliation: that God was reconciling the world to himself in Christ, not counting people's sins against them. And He has committed to **us** the message of reconciliation. We are therefore Christ's ambassadors, as though God were making his appeal through us. We implore you on Christ's behalf: Be reconciled to God. (2 Corinthians 5:11, 18-20)

What ministry has God given to every believer?

_____

_____

What is the message He has commissioned us to spread?

_____

_____

What kind of emotion does Paul display here, towards the lost?

_____

What kind of attitude does the Father have about reaching His sheep?

_____

_____

For everyone who calls on the name of the Lord will be saved. But how then will they call on Him in whom they have not believed? And how are they to believe in Him of whom they have never heard? How are they to hear without someone preaching? And how are they to preach unless they are sent? As it is written,

"How beautiful are the feet of those who preach the good news!" (Romans 10:13-15)

How many people are required to reach an entire globe, for Christ?

_____

Why are the "feet" of missionaries called "beautiful"?

_____

If you don't evangelize, who are some people around you who might die without hearing?

_____

_____

Truly, truly, I say to you, **whoever believes in me** will also do the works that I do; and greater works than these will he do, because I am going to the Father. (John 14:12)

Does Jesus expect all His followers to evangelize?

_____

Does Jesus give us reason to be hopeful or doubtful about our evangelism?

_____

_____

Then He said to his disciples, "The harvest is plentiful, but the laborers are few; therefore pray earnestly to the Lord of the harvest to send out laborers into his harvest." (Matthew 9:37-38)

What did Jesus say His followers should pray for? Why?

_____

_____

How can we help answer this prayer?

_____

Standing Strong

Therefore do not be ashamed of the testimony about our Lord, nor of me his prisoner, but share in suffering for the gospel by the power of God, who saved us and called us to a holy calling. (2 Timothy 1:9)

Will you come under pressure and attack if you evangelize?

_____

How does God want you to react?

_____

_____

For I am not ashamed of the gospel, for it is the power of God for salvation to everyone who believes, to the Jew first and also to the Greek. (Romans 1:16)

If you are not ashamed of the gospel, how will you witness to others?

_____

_____

Does Jesus want you only to evangelize privately or to your friends?

_____

_____

What kinds of things do Christians do, which show that they are ashamed of the Truth?

_____

_____

_____

You therefore must endure hardness as a good soldier of Jesus Christ. No one engaged in warfare entangles himself with the affairs of this life, that he may please him who enlisted him as a soldier. And also if anyone competes in athletics, he is not crowned unless he competes according to the rules. Pray also for me, that whenever I speak, words may be given me so that I will fearlessly make known the mystery of the gospel, for which I am an ambassador in chains that I may declare it boldly, as I ought to speak. (Ephesians 6:19-20)

What kind of attitude do you need to reach out with the gospel?

_____

_____

What will happen if you get distracted by the things of the world?

_____

_____

How does God feel about you hiding your witness? What if you are punished for it?

_____

"When they persecute you in one town, flee to the next..." (Matthew 5:23)
"And you will be hated by all for my name's sake. But the one who endures to the end will be saved." (Matthew 5:22)

Why is it hard to be an evangelist?

_____

As you enter the house, greet it. And if the house is worthy, let your peace come upon it, but if it is not worthy, let your peace return to you. And if anyone will not receive you or listen to your words, shake off the dust from your feet when you leave that house or town. Truly, I say to you, it will be more bearable on the day of judgment for the land of Sodom and Gomorrah than for that town. (Matthew 10: 5-15)

Jesus says our job is to preach the truth. Which two ways will people respond to this?

_____

_____

Are you supposed to let it bother you when people reject you? Or reject the gospel?

_____

FINDING YOUR PLACE
Joining the Battle

> When our enemies heard that we knew what they were going to do, and that God had frustrated their plan, we all returned to the wall, each to his work. From that day on, half of my servants worked on construction, and half held the spears, shields, bows, and coats of mail. And the leaders stood behind the whole house of Judah who were building on the wall... (Nehemiah 4:15-16)

Nehemiah was charged with rebuilding the walls of Jerusalem after the city had been torn down. Did everyone all have the same job?

_____

Think of rebuilding a wall like building God's Kingdom. Do Christians all have the same job in building God's Kingdom today?

_____

Think about the different people involved in bringing you to know Jesus. List some different roles they played.

_____

_____

_____

List some other ways you see Christians actively involved in society today.

_____

_____

_____

Nehemiah's wall would have been very large. How does everyone doing their piece help build and protect the city of God?

_____

_____

Those who carried burdens were loaded in such a way that each labored on the work with one hand and held his weapon with the other. And each of the builders had his sword strapped at his side while he built. (Nehemiah 4:17-18)

What were the two things each person stationed on the wall had?

_____

_____

What were the two aspects to their job?

_____

_____

Did it matter where each person on the wall was? Did their general job description differ?

_____

What were the two results of each person taking their place?

_____

_____

Then Jesus came to them and said, "All authority in heaven and on earth has been given to me. Therefore go and make disciples of all nations, baptizing them in the name of the Father and of the Son and of the Holy Spirit, and teaching them to obey everything I have commanded you. And surely I am with you always, to the very end of the age. (Matthew 28:18-20)

If God's mission is to disciple the nations, can any one job do it all?

_____

Can any one person or any one Christian ministry do all the jobs required?

_____

If you are dedicated to obeying the gospel, what do you end up doing, no matter what you do?

_____

Does Jesus tell His disciples what to do, to fulfill this Great Commission?

_____

Do you need to wait for your particular destiny to be revealed, such as in a prophecy or a timetable you create for yourself?

_____

_____

> As it is, there are many parts, but one body. The eye cannot say to the hand, "I don't need you!" And the head cannot say to the feet, "I don't need you!" On the contrary, those parts of the body that seem to be weaker are indispensable, and the parts we think are less honorable are treated with special honor...
>
> God has put the Body together, giving greater honor to the parts that lacked it so that there should be no division in the Body, but that its parts should have equal concern for each other. If one part suffers, every part suffers with it; if one part is honored, every part rejoices with it. Now you are the Body of Christ, and each one of you is a part of it.   (1 Corinthians 12:20-27)

How many parts of your physical body are there? Which parts are not needed?

_____

_____

Who has put the Body of Christ—the Church—together?

_____

Are there parts of God's Kingdom that you are not interested in building? (Business, Politics, Education, Arts/Entertainment...??) What would happen if Christians refused to enter one of these parts of society?

_____

_____

What happens when Christians enter them?

_____

_____

_____

How should we feel when a different group of Christians pursues something with excellence and results? Even when their cause doesn't resonate with us personally?

_____

_____

Have you seen Christians shooting themselves with "friendly fire"? In what ways have you seen them do that?

_____

_____

_____

_____

Pray and ask God to reveal any area where you believe or behave in a way that is like "friendly fire."

_____

_____

_____

Whatever You Do

> Whatever your hand finds to do, do it with all your might. (Ecclesiastes 9:10)
> Whatever you do, do it all for the glory of God. (1 Corinthians 10:31)

Do these verses make it sound as if there is just one valid job in the Kingdom?

_____

_____

What two things are more important than the job you choose?

_____

_____

Consider the statement that "The problem you see is the problem you're called to fix." How is this Scriptural?

_____

_____

_____

> Whatever you do, work heartily as for the Lord and not for men. (Colossians 3:23).

Is your mission in life really about you?

_____

List a few ways that the world trains you to think about men more than the Lord, when you work.

_____

_____

_____

Does Scripture exhort you to spend lots of time trying to pinpoint your specific purpose or calling?

_____

_____

Will you miss God's best, if you don't figure it all out early in life?

_____

_____

> While the people were listening to this, Jesus proceeded to tell them a parable, because He was near Jerusalem and they thought the kingdom of God would appear imminently. So He said, "A man of noble birth went to a distant country to lay claim to his kingship and then return. Beforehand, he called ten of his servants and gave them ten minas. 'Conduct business with this until I return,' he said... When he returned from procuring his kingship, he summoned the servants to whom he had given the money, to find out what each one had earned. The first servant came forward and said, 'Master, your mina has produced ten more

minas.' His master replied, 'Well done, good servant! Because you have been faithful in a very small matter, you shall have authority over ten cities.' The second servant came and said, 'Master, your mina has made five minas. 'And to this one he said, 'You shall have authority over five cities.'

Then another servant came and said, 'Master, here is your mina, which I have laid away in a piece of cloth. For I was afraid of you, because you are a harsh man. You withdraw what you did not deposit and reap what you did not sow.' His master replied, 'You wicked servant, I will judge you by your own words. So you knew that I am a harsh man, withdrawing what I did not deposit and reaping what I did not sow? Why then did you not deposit my money in the bank, and upon my return I could have collected it with interest?'

Then he told those standing by, 'Take the mina from him and give it to the one who has ten minas' 'Master,' they said, 'he already has ten!' He replied, 'I tell you that everyone who has will be given more; but the one who does not have, even what he has will be taken away from him..." (Luke 19:11-19)

Why did Jesus tell the crowds this parable about investing their resources? What point about the Kingdom's finality was He trying to make?

_____

_____

What did the master tell each servant, to whom He gave money?

_____

_____

Did the master tell each servant what to do? Did he give any specific instructions?

_____

_____

What was the main thing the master was hoping each servant would do?

_____

Why did the servant who hid the money, hide it?

_____

_____

What will keep you from investing yourself in God's Kingdom?

_____

_____

Does God control the activity or timing with which you do everything for Him? Who has authority over that?

_____

What reward did the master give, for the servants' investment? What was he looking to give away?

_____

What will you be given as a reward for your authority over yourself and your own good decisions when you invest in His Kingdom on earth?

_____

_____

Using What You Have: Moses

Moses answered, "What if they [the Egyptians] do not believe me or listen to me and say, 'The Lord did not appear to you'?" Then the Lord said to him, "What is that in your hand?" "A staff," he replied. The Lord said, "Throw it on the ground..." Moses threw it on the ground and it became a snake, and he ran from it. Then the Lord said to him, "Reach out your hand and take it by the tail." So Moses reached out and took hold of the snake and it turned back into a staff in his hand. "This," said the Lord, "is so that they may believe that the Lord, the God of their fathers—the God of Abraham, the God of Isaac and the God of Jacob—has appeared to you."

Then the Lord said, "Put your hand inside your cloak." So Moses put his hand into his cloak, and when he took it out, the skin was leprous —it had become as white as snow. "Now put it back into your cloak," he said. So Moses put his hand back into his cloak, and when he took it out, it was restored, like the rest of his flesh.

Then the Lord said, "If they do not believe you or pay attention to the first sign, they may believe the second. But if they do not believe these two signs or listen to you, take some water from the Nile and pour it on the dry ground. The water you take from the river will become blood on the ground..." Moses said to the Lord, "Pardon your servant, Lord. I have never been eloquent, neither in the past

nor since you have spoken to your servant. I am slow of speech and tongue."
The Lord said to him, "Who gave human beings their mouths? Who makes them
deaf or mute? Who gives them sight or makes them blind? Is it not I, the Lord?
Now go; I will help you speak and will teach you what to say." (Exodus 4:1-13)

How did God respond to Moses' feelings that he was not qualified or able to fight?

_____

_____

Moses was a shepherd with a simple staff in his hands. What did God use as his
weapon?

_____

God used what Moses already had "in his hand" to defeat Egypt. What background,
training, or personality traits do you already have "in your hand?"

_____

_____

_____

Have you rejected anything God has put in your hands as not fantastic enough to be
used by Him?

_____

_____

Do you need to have special training, followers, or formidable equipment to make a
difference for God?

_____

Does God intend to back you up when you go out to fight? What can you rely on?

_____

Does your mission have to fit your natural strengths?

_____

Does your mission have to fulfill everything you've ever dreamed of?

_____

After 400 years of enslavement under Pharaoh, God had a problem He needed fixing and Moses was swept into that. What problems does God have right now, that need fixing right around you?

_____

_____

_____

> But Moses said, "Pardon your servant, Lord. Please send someone else. Then the Lord's anger burned against Moses and he said, "What about your brother, Aaron the Levite? I know he can speak well. He is already on his way to meet you, and he will be glad to see you. You shall speak to him and put words in his mouth; I will help both of you speak and will teach you what to do. He will speak to the people for you, and it will be as if he were your mouth and as if you were God to him. But take this staff in your hand so you can perform the signs with it." (Exodus 4:14-17).

Does God like it when He wants us to go for Him, but we won't?

_____

Does God see your limitations as His own limitations?

_____

Why doesn't having real limitations give you an excuse not to fight where He needs you?

_____

_____

Was God able to solve Moses' inadequacy problems?

_____

Did God take away His approval, His mission, or His love from Moses just because Moses hesitated? Why not?

_____

_____

Accepting Your Piece: David

God said to me [King David], "You shall not build a house for My name because you are a man of war and have shed blood." Yet the Lord, the God of Israel, chose me from all the house of my father to be king over Israel forever. For He has chosen Judah to be a leader; and in the house of Judah, my father's house, and among the sons of my father He took pleasure in me to make me king over all Israel. (1 Chronicles 2:3-4)

David was not allowed to build God's Temple because he was a warrior and had shed blood. Yet he expressed that he was beloved by God anyway as the King of Judah. Did this bother David? Why not?

_____

_____

Does God want you to wish you were someone else, with different talents or passions?

_____

_____

David and Joshua were both warriors. Joseph and Daniel were foreign advisers. Abraham and Moses met with God personally in the wilderness. Did God intend everyone to serve Him in the same ways? What does He understand about His mission?

_____

_____

Can you accept your unique piece of His mission?

_____

_____

Write down any thoughts you have about what that might look like in this season of your life.

_____

_____

www.ingramcontent.com/pod-product-compliance
Lightning Source LLC
Chambersburg PA
CBHW082005060426
42449CB00037B/3409